If Quetzals Could Cry

A Guatemalan Scrapbook
with Designs for Worship

Dondeena Caldwell

Friendship Press • New York

Friendship Press is grateful to publishers and photographers for permission to reprint quotes, poems, articles and pictures. For publishing information, permissions and credits, please see the Index to Sources, pages 77-79, the list of Illustrations, page 76, and the Footnotes, pages 79-80.

Layout and design: Carol Görgün

Library of Congress Cataloging-in-Publication Data
Caldwell, Dondeena, 1927 -
    If Quetzals could cry : a Guatemalan scrapbook with designs for worship /
Dondeena Caldwell.
        p. cm.
    Includes bibliographical references.
    ISBN 0-377-00206-2
    1. Mayas—Folklore. 2. Mayas—Religion and mythology. 3. Mayas-Poetry.
4. Human rights—Guatemala. 5. Guatemala—Social conditions. I. Title.
F1435.3.F6C35 1990
972.81'016—dc20   89-49102

ISBN 0-377-00206-2
Editorial Office: 475 Riverside Drive, Room 772, New York, NY 10115
Distribution Office: P.O. Box 37844, Cincinnati, OH 45222-0844

Contents

Photo: Pat Goodvis

Introduction

A headline in the *Los Angeles Times* on September 26, 1989, announced: "Rightists Blamed for Wave of Violence in Guatemala." Marjorie Miller, the *Times* staff writer, reported, "Alleged right-wing extremists have unleashed a campaign of kidnappings, assassinations, and bombings in the worst wave of violence to strike Guatemala since civilian President Vinicio Cerezo Arévalo took office nearly four years ago."

Roman Catholic bishops were quoted: "Guatemala does not want to and does not deserve to live another horrendous experience." Yet the Episcopal Conference of Guatemala reports a "feeling of desperation and fear" in the country.

How has Guatemala reached such a crisis? Indeed, how has the "land of eternal spring" survived the crises that began in the sixteenth century when the Spaniards arrived with muskets and measles? In spite of the Conquest and subsequent centuries of exploitation, descendants of the original inhabitants of Guatemala, the Mayas, still outnumber European descendants in much of their homeland. Mayas have managed to preserve the threads of their tradition that persevere as strong and bright as those of the beautiful Guatemalan textiles still woven by hand today.

The exquisite costume designs tell a silent story of a culture that goes back three thousand years. Silent also is the national symbol of Guatemala, the quetzal, one of the world's most beautiful birds. According to legend, the quetzal lost its voice when the Spaniards arrived. And some have called Guatemala itself the "silent country." Thousands upon thousands of Guatemalans have suffered injustices in stoic silence year after year.

Those suffering injustice are beginning to break the silence by speaking out against the military and the economic elite who oppose any movement of social change. Among those no longer silent are some leaders of the Roman Catholic and mainline Protestant churches, as well as labor leaders, teachers, students, and organizations of indigenous groups.

1

The beleaguered Guatemalans are also confronted with apathy and ignorance about them among their neighbors to the north, the United States and Canada. If such conditions continue, the people of Guatemala have little chance of achieving lasting economic and political security or human dignity.

Our ignorance of the shocking, tragic facts of what is happening to the Guatemalan people prevails because much information goes unreported in our media. Most of us have been kept in the dark about such atrocities as the destruction of hundreds of villages, the widespread hunger in the cities, and the rampant homelessness. Neither do we hear of the virtual genocide of the Mayan Indians, their continual danger, and their uneven struggles against ruthless military power coupled with rightist business interests.

If quetzals could cry, they would cry out against the existing conditions in Guatemala. They would call out to us, joining the over one hundred priests, pastors, theologians, and laypersons, many from Guatemala, who signed the *Kairos: Central America* document on April 3, 1988. Part of it reads:

> *We are your neighbors.* We want to give you our answer to that question that perhaps you, like the Scribe in the Gospel, have been asking, "Who is my neighbor?"(Luke 10:25ff). We are that "certain man" in Jesus' parable for whom you must be good Samaritans. We are wounded by the roadside, enslaved without pity by successive empires, exploited by the transnationals, repressed and massacred by military apparatuses, deprived of life's most fundamental things, deported, exiles, refugees. . . . Even though distant from you geographically, we are very close to you. So close as a matter of fact as to be the reverse side of your own situation. We are your neighbors. Do not turn a deaf ear to Central America's cry. Do not walk by on the other side, even if it is to go to church. Do not be afraid to contaminate yourselves by taking up our cause. Rather, listen to Jesus' word, "inasmuch as you did it to my smallest brothers and sisters, you did it to me . . ." (Matthew 25:31ff).

> It is no longer possible to be a Christian shut up in the narrow confines of one's own community, or country. Today the only way to be consistent in our Christianity is to take seriously our historical international responsibility with regard to our world neighbors. The cosmos is our home. The world is our responsibility. Collective history is our task. It is there that we must make our passionate cry, "Come, Lord Jesus."[1]

How to use this book

The book can be read prayerfully in silence and solitude, or it can be used as a source for group meditation, discussion, and action. Each chapter begins with an introduction to be shared with the group as background for understanding the readings. Spend much time in prayer during preparations for the presentation of the material. After considering each theme with the group, discuss new insights and ways to stand in solidarity with our sisters and brothers in Guatemala. As eyes are opened to the beauty of Guatemala and its people, may they recognize the resilience and strength of those who have suffered for centuries.

A few guidelines for planning worship

1. If possible, read the entire book to get the "feel" of the whole, rather than its parts. Choose readings, Scripture passages—from those suggested and others—that will fit the time and goals of your group. Using suggestions in "Meditations" section of each chapter, arrange the room you are using with appropriate symbols and center for worship and plan for the use of music.

2. Involve as many people as possible as participants. Encourage each person to share ideas and information.

3. Allow those who will participate in each session sufficient time to prepare in order to make each poem, story, or body of information most effective.

4. If possible, ask someone fluent in Spanish to read some of the poetry in Spanish in order to capture the "feel" of the language of many in Guatemala.

5. Prepare copies of and distribute information on page 74 for further study, involvement, and action in the human rights struggle in Guatemala. (Other material in this book is copyright by Friendship Press and other publishers, so should not be reproduced without permission.)

Note: Most of the poetry in this book that was originally in Spanish, as well as some prose stories and interviews, have been translated by Dondeena Caldwell.

3

Clearing land to plant corn in the
highland village of Chajul.
Descendants of the Maya still
revere the earth and pray for its
forgiveness before tilling the land.
Photo: Derrill Bazzy, 1985

ONE
The Sacred Land of the Mayas

The quetzal disappears into mountain jungle. The bird's body glistens like Mayan jade with brilliant green and blue feathers and an iridescent red breast. Its tail, from two to three feet long, trails in a graceful question mark. This streamer-trailing beauty takes its name from *quetzalli*, an Aztec word for tail feather, which came to mean "precious" or "beautiful."[1]

But today the quetzal is close to extinction. It is losing its habitat because the forests are being cut and burned and its life because its rare feathers are sold illegally. The quetzal's survival is threatened, much as is the survival of Mayan Indians and their descendants. Centuries ago they lost their lands to the Spanish Conquest; now their lands are eaten up by forever-encroaching big business interests and greedy landowners. Loss of what was their ancestral home disrupts life. Becoming the human fodder for the system of putting more money in fewer pockets results in perpetual poverty, if not extinction, to many Indians.

No wonder the quetzal has no voice to sing, and no wonder a strain of melancholy pervades every composition of true Indian music, no matter for what purpose it is played or sung.[2] Though Indian melodies are heartsobs, the words often speak of the people's love for the land and its beauty.

Mayan music's profound feeling for nature grows out of the belief that the land and what it produces is sacred. The soil of Guatemala, rich from volcanic ash, provided the nourishment for *teocintle*, the wild-grass ancestor of maize and corn. By 1000 B.C., nomadic groups called Maya lived in the forests of what is now the Department of Petén and harvested the primitive grains.[3]

These Indians inhabited both mountains and valleys. Although they developed twenty-two different dialects, they shared an adoration of nature. One object of their veneration was the ceiba tree. Village leaders used to meet under the ceiba tree, which they called the "tree of counsel." Since it usually is in the center of an Indian village, the ceiba offers its shade for everyone during market day. Three or more crosses under a giant ceiba tree indicate the presence of an Indian medicine man, called a shaman, who can also tell fortunes.[4]

Crops and ceiba trees still thrive in the fertile soil of Guatemala, a country slightly larger than the State of Tennessee in the United States and twice as large as Nova Scotia in Canada. The rolling hills and mountains, considered to be the sacred dwelling places of Indian Ancestors, are always green, the color of eternal springtime. The verdant growth and the land on which it grows are sacred, yet few places demonstrate more spectacularly the violence of nature. One of the world's most active volcanic chains, with more than one hundred major volcanoes, begins at the northern border of Guatemala and ends in Panama.[5] Of the thirty-seven Guatemalan volcanoes in this "circle of fire," eight are still active.[6]

The first recorded cataclysm happened in 1541, when the water in Agua's crater cascaded down the mountainside and demolished Ciudad Viejo, the capital of the country newly colonized by Spain. One victim of the catastrophe was the widow of Pedro de Alvarado, conquerer of Guatemala.[7] But the Mayas see the coming of the Spaniards and the subsequent foreign intervention as more devastating than volcanic eruptions.

Guatemala, the ancestral home of the Mayas, is eternally beautiful, eternally sacred, as are those people who live within her borders.

Meditation

Music: Music, an international language, unites people of different backgrounds and experiences. The Indians of Guatemala were attracted to the Bible stories that the Spaniards set to simple music. Similarly, the Spaniards drew upon existing Mayan musical styles and instruments.

One such instrument, the marimba, is typical of Guatemala. Though its origin is African, a form of the marimba existed long before the arrival in Central America of either white or black people. The Indians played on a string of gourds tied around their waists. They played the gourds with two sticks tipped with rubber.[8]

The marimba's soft sighs and sobbing scales speak of lost loves and lost dreams and of hope reborn. Play marimba music softly while the scripture selection is read. (Two sources of this music are: "Marimba from Oaxaca," Folkways Co. #8865, and "Music of Guatemala," Folkways Co. #4212.)

Scripture Passage: Psalm 148:1-14 (A song of praise to God).

Reflection: How does the Psalmist look at nature? Compare the Israelites with the Mayas and their reverence for the land.

Readings: Choose several of the selections in the Readings section.

Affirm: The "holy shrine" and people of every land, especially Guatemala, by singing the "Song of Peace" (to the tune *Finlandia*; words by Lloyd Stone, published by Lorenz Publishing Co.).

The Ceiba of My Town

Like all the towns of my land
mine has a ceiba, beautiful and noble;
higher than the mahogany tree
and stronger than the oak.

It has lived for centuries
like the ancient church
in front of which it extends its foliage;
and it looks like another temple,
with its green dome
and a musical belltower of birds!

Curtained with the sun in the morning,
and at night with half-moon-shaped veils,
when wandering lightning bugs light it
with a thousand necklaces of little green bulbs.

—Angelina Acuña

La Ceiba de Mi Pueblo

Como todos los pueblos de mi tierra
tiene el mío una ceiba, hermosa y noble;
más alta que el caobo
y más fuerte que el roble.

Ha vivido centenios
como la antigua iglesia
frente a la cual, extiende su follaje;
y parece otro templo,
con su cúpula verde
y un campanario musical de pájaros!

Se encortina de sol por la mañana
y por la noche de lunados velos,
cuando errantes luciérnagas la alumbran
con mil collares de foquitos verdes.

—Angelina Acuña
from *Poemas Escogidos para Niños*

Monja Blanca

Mariposa rara
de nieve y rocío
nació en la montaña
temblando de frío.

Dulce Monja Blanca
mi Flor Nacional;
mariposa rara
de la Verapaz.

Vestida de blanco
flor de la montaña;
símbolo y encanto
de mi Guatemala.

—Adrián Ramírez Flores
from *Poemas Escogidos para Niños*

La Ceiba

Florón de gloria en aldeana plaza
imagen de lo grande y lo sublime
que el alma noble eleva y la redime
de lo pequeño, que su ser desplaza.

Refugio de avecilla cantadora,
o de viajero que a su tronco llega
y del romero que en el templo ruega:
florido arpegio del que canta y ora.

Con razón te escogió la patria
por excelsa en el reino vegetal:
si grandeza, bonanza y armonía

es de tu ser la esencia prodigiosa:
la savia de tu mole colosal.
Eres más que princesa o reina, diosa.

—Julián Méndez Hidalgo
from *Poemas Escogidos para Niños*

Monja Blanca (White Nun)*

Rare butterfly
of snow and dew
born in the mountain
shivering with cold.

Sweet White Nun
my national flower;
rare butterfly
of Verapaz.

Dressed in white,
flower of the mountain;
symbol and enchantment
of my Guatemala.

—Adrián Ramírez Flores
* Guatemala's national flower, called "White Nun"

The Ceiba

Huge flower of glory in village plaza,
image of the great and the sublime
that elevates the noble soul and redeems it
from the littleness that its being displaces.

Refuge for the little singing bird,
or for the traveler who arrives at your trunk
and for the pilgrim who prays in the temple:
flowery arpeggio from one who sings and prays.

No wonder our country chose you
for your excellence in the plant kingdom:
Yes, greatness, goodness, and harmony

is the marvellous essence of your being:
the vital fluid of your colossal size.
You are more than princess or queen;
you are a goddess.

—Julián Méndez Hidalgo

A Guatemala

Dulce tierra solar, de piel oscura,
dulce tierra caliente, a nadie extraña
yo amo desde tu seno de montaña,
hasta el húmedo pie de tu llanura!

El Océano que abraza tu cintura
hecho torrente, se internó en tu entraña
y en la lluvia y el río que te baña,
madre, joven, mantiene tu frescura.

Se inclina hasta besar tu piel morena
un cielo azul, traslúcido y sereno:
la montaña te hincha, como llena
un suave cuerpo femenil el seno
y vas preñada de la dulce pena
de un pardo vientre eternamente lleno.

—Rafael Arévalo Martínez
from Poemas Escogidos para Niños

To Guatemala

Sweet ancestor-dwelling, with dark skin,
Sweet warm earth, who rejects no one,
I love you from the bosom of your mountains
to the humid feet of your plains!

The ocean that embraces your waist
becomes a torrent, sinks into your depths
and in the rain and in the river bathes you,
youthful mother, and maintains your freshness.

Bending over until kissing your dark skin
a blue sky, translucent and serene;
the mountains inflate you, like
the soft feminine body fills the breast
and you go pregnant with the sweet pain
of a brown womb eternally full.

—Rafael Arévalo Martínez

Himno Nacional (Selected verses)

Reposing in the lofty Andes,
from two seas a sonorous noise,
under the wing of golden grain
you are lulled by the beautiful quetzal.

Indian bird that lives on your coat of arms,
Guardian that protects your land;
May your flight soar
higher than the condor or royal eagle.

—José Joaquín Palma

Always Our Home

We have always lived here: we have the right to go on living where we are happy and where we want to die. Only here can we feel whole; nowhere else would we ever feel complete and our pain would be eternal.

—Diego Reinoso, from Popol Vuh*
quoted in I, Rigoberta Menchú

* See page 13.

15 de Septiembre (Independence Day)*

Beautiful date, the nation
raises its noble banner
and everyone smiles and sings
at the feet of this banner.

It wasn't the roaring cannon,
nor the exalted warrior
who in fierce battle
gave us independence:
It was the law of conscience
and not the sharp edge of steel.

Without stupid rage,
without deep animosity,
we said goodbye to each other serenely
from the encircling arms of Spain.
And the hate that tarnishes the soul
did not follow this act;
the two nations, the two
who would form a strong bond,
united in tender embrace
and bid each other goodbye.

> —Máximo Soto Hall
> from *Poemas Escogidos para Niños*

* Spain ruled Central America from 1524 to 1821, when on September 15
  Guatemala, without warfare, declared its independence.

TWO
From Corn Paste to Kings

Shortly after the conquest of the area that became Guatemala by Spain in 1524, Diego Reinoso, a Quiché Indian, wrote a history of the origin of his people, the *Popol Vuh*. He wrote in his own language, using Spanish alphabet letters, and he blended pre- and post-conquest beliefs. He not only repeated the story of Adam and Eve, but made it four times better.[1] In his account the Indian gods created four Adams from corn paste, the substance of life for the Indians. Then each received an Eve.

Before the coming of the Spaniards, the Mayas developed arts and sciences as well as agriculture. Their religious and civil ceremonies included music and dance. They painted and sculpted, decorating everything from pots to temples. They perfected an ideographic system for writing with symbols and also a simple numerical system of dots and dashes that was two thousand years ahead of the general use of mathematics in Europe. Their use of zero antedated that of the Arabs by a millennium.[2]

The "people made of corn paste" prospered and had no reason to believe that their "garden of Eden" would become a "killing field." Tecún Umán, the chief among the lords of Utatlán, the Quiché capital, had received a warning from Mexico about the Spanish and their great military power. The last Aztec ruler there, Moctezuma, had sent word that Pedro de Alvarado was on his way to Guatemala with three hundred Spanish infantrymen. When they arrived, they routed the Quiché army. Spanish chronicles credit Alvarado himself with killing Tecún Umán, the Quiché king.[3]

"When Alvarado's mercenaries slaughtered some 30,000 Mayans on the battlefield of Quetzaltenango, so the legend goes, countless quetzals flew down to earth from heaven and formed a deathwatch, covering the dead Indians with the feathers of the birds, and since then, say the Guatemalan Indians, the quetzal is red on its underside."[4]

Each Indian's life was identified with an animal guardian. The spirit's counterpart, the *nagual*, of Tecún Umán was the quetzal. The legend is that while Alvarado and the Quiché chief fought hand-to-hand, Alvarado

Watched by a member of the Guatemalan civilian patrol, women in the village of Ixcan wait their turns to grind corn for tortillas.
Photo: Derrill Bazzy, 1989

really killed the quetzal that appeared above the Indian's head.

Some say that the quetzal lost its voice when the Spaniards defeated the Mayas. Others say it never lost its voice, but has since refused to sing.[5]

Such legends offer insight into the Mayan psyche and into the Mayan heritage that colors and shapes Guatemala. The inclusion of a quetzal on the Guatemalan flag symbolizes freedom and reflects the belief that quetzals cannot live in captivity.

Half of Guatemala's inhabitants are Indian. Of the other half, more than eighty percent have some Indian ancestry.[6] To understand the Indian perspective is to understand Guatemala.

Meditation

Background and Setting: God miraculously supplied food to the Hebrew people as they wandered through the wilderness. Called manna, that nourishing staple was their life-sustaining food. We think of that "staff of life" as bread, but the Indians of Guatemala would consider manna to be maize, or corn. The Hebrews were cautioned against hoarding their manna, and the Mayan Indians teach their children to share.

Indian children learn to respect corn, their symbol of life, and to care for it. Any grain dropped on the ground must be picked up for planting or for food. They also learn that they, like grains of corn, will multiply the race, replacing those who have died.

On a table arrange ears of corn and other corn products, such as corn meal, tortillas, hominy, or corn starch. This display represents the main source of food in the diet of many Guatemalans. Every grain of maize is valued as representing life. Children are taught that they are made of maize because their mothers ate it while pregnant.

Scripture Passages: Ask those reading the following passages to substitute "corn" for "bread."

Psalm 132:15 (Satisfy the poor with bread).

Proverbs 22:19 (Share bread with the poor).

Matthew 6:11 (Give us bread).

Symbolic Action: *Sharing the food of Guatemala.* Kneel together in a circle. Sing "Let Us Break Bread Together on Our Knees" using the words, "Let Us Share Corn Together." While singing each person will, in turn, tear off a piece of tortilla, and share it with the person to the right.

End with a prayer that people and nations will learn to share rather than selfishly hoard or consume food, land, material wealth, and God's love.

(For the next session, ask people to bring individual pictures of family members and relatives.)

Readings

Creation Story

Everything was in suspense, calm, silent. Not a single person existed, neither animals, nor birds, fish, crabs, trees, rocks, valleys, precipices, meadows, or cornfields. The surface of the earth was not visible, only the tranquil sea. In the silence of the dark night the gods were surrounded by a brilliant light. They were covered with shawls, green as a quetzal.

. . . They decided how to express their thoughts and feelings. "Let the waters part so the earth can be worked, and may its surface be like a plate. May the light be born so the future inhabitants of the earth will be able to see in order to plant food to eat," they all said. When they shouted, "Earth!" something supernatural, strange, and marvelous happened as mountains formed, coastlines appeared, and valleys were covered with cypress and pine trees.

They cut out channels for rivers and made the animals that would live in the waters, the birds, lions and tigers of the jungles, and the rattlesnakes and big snakes destined to live under tropical growth. To all, the gods indicated what to do in order to live. They said, "Call on us, worship us, because we made you."

None of the animals could say the names of the gods. "What can we do so the animals can call on us and invoke our names as the greatest on earth?" the gods said. They began to make flesh from wet clay, but realized that the clay would dissolve.

They made wooden dolls that looked like people. But these wooden beings had no heart or feelings, nor did they recognize that they were children of the gods. The gods prepared to destroy them with a thick rain that would completely cover the earth.

Then the gods tried to form people, looking for the right kind of flesh. Four animals brought news about yellow and white ears of grain. From those grains the goddess Ixmucané made nine drinks, and from them formed the first men. Great was the wisdom of those first four men. After they had seen everything under the sun, they thanked the gods three times.

The gods, who were pleased, made the men fall asleep. When they awoke, they found four beautiful women who filled their hearts with happiness. These eight gave origin to many large and small towns.

—Adapted from *Popol Vuh*[7]

El Quetzal

Alado pensamiento de colores
que arcoirisa el azul con tardo vuelo,
condensación crepuscular del cielo,
alma de pedrerías y de flores.

Augur de los altivos gladiadores
que defendieron palmo a palmo el suelo,
cuando envolvió a la América el anhelo
devastador de los conquistadores.

Estuche de esmeraldas y rubíes,
redondos ojos como puntos de íes
que se encienden en bélica amenaza.

La libertad bajo sus alas vuela,
y en su augusto silencio se revela
la infinita tristeza de la raza.

—Félix Calderón Avila
from *Poemas Escogidos para Niños*

The Quetzal

Winged thought in colors
that rainbows the blue in slow flight,
dawn's dew from heaven,
soul of precious stones and flowers.

Augur of proud gladiators
that defended their land hand-to-hand,
when the devastating ambition of conquerors
enveloped America.

Jewel case of emeralds and rubies,
round eyes like the dots of i's
flaming in warlike threat.

Freedom flies under your wings
and in your magnificent silence is revealed
the infinite sadness of the race.

—Félix Calderón Avila

Razones del Maíz

La patria es de maíz.
Su aliento viene desde lejos,
desde que Ixmucané—diosa transida—
molió el grano vital y modeló a los hombres,
a los cuatro primeros capitanes
de nuestra estirpe maya,
padres y dirigentes de nuestra sangre antigua
y edificadores de las cuatro columnas
que sostienen el cielo.

Por eso es que en la noche
los granos de maíz
cintilan como estrellas.

Los antiguos señores dedicaron su vida
a cincelar encajes con el oro y la plata,
a sorber espumosas bebidas de cacao
y a labrar una inmensa alegría de maizales.

Por eso es que en la sangre
de la gente de ahora
el maíz se convierte en llamarada.

> —Otto-raúl Gonzaléz
> from *Poemas Escogidos para Niños*

The Birth of a Child

The child is to be part of the community. The birth of a new member is very significant for the community, as it belongs to the community, not just to the parents, and that's why three couples (but not just anybody) must be there to receive it. They explain that this child is the fruit of communal love. . . .

Our people feel that the baby's school must be the community itself, that [the child] must learn to live like all the rest of us. The tying of the hands at birth also symbolizes this: that no one should accumulate things the rest of the community does not have and [one] must know how to share, to have open hands.

> —Rigoberta Menchú,* from *I, Rigoberta Menchú*

Reason for Corn

The country is made from corn.
Your breath comes from long ago,
since Ixmucané, the grief-stricken goddess,
ground the vital grain and molded men,
the first four captains
of our Mayan race,
fathers and leaders of the blood of our past,
and builders of the four columns
that hold up the heavens.

This is why in the night
the grains of corn
shine like stars.

The ancient lords dedicated their life
to chisel inlaid work with gold and silver,
to sip foaming drinks of cocoa
and to cultivate immense cornfields of happiness.

For that reason in the blood
of the people today
corn becomes a flame of fire.

                —Otto-raúl González

---

* Rigoberta Menchú is a young Guatemalan peasant woman, already famous in her country as a national leader. Faced with gross injustice and exploitation, she decided to learn Spanish as an adult, even though she had never gone to school. She became a Roman Catholic catechist, as much as an expression of social revolt as of her deep religious belief. After the coming to power of the Lucas Garcia regime in 1978, her brother, father, and mother were all killed in separate, horrifying incidents on the part of the army. Rigoberta tells her story, which reflects the common experiences of many Indian communities in Latin America, to another Latin American woman, Elisabeth Burgos-Debray, an anthropologist.

God of Thunder and Lightning

Cortez* was received in a cordial manner by Canek, the ruler of Tayasal. . . . Upon his departure, Cortez was forced to leave behind a horse crippled by a stake that had penetrated its foot; the animal became the central figure in the strange Indian legend of Tzimin Char.

The Petén Itza held horses in great reverence, as did most other Indians throughout the conquered regions of Mexico and Central America. To them the horse was the living symbol of the great and awesome power of the Spaniard. When the Maya of Tayasal were unexpectedly presented with one, the worshipful Indians made offerings of flowers and poultry concoctions to the poor beast, who soon died from the unusual diet. In commemoration, a stone statue was erected to the animal and placed in one of the great temples, where it was thereafter worshipped as Tzimin Char, the god of thunder and lightning.

—from *The View from the Top of the Temple*

* The Spaniards captured Nito, a Mayan port near the Yucatan Pennisula, but could barely make a living in the jungle. In 1524, Cortez led an overland expedition from Mexico City to check on the area. He returned to Mexico by sea.[8]

THREE
If Quetzals Could Cry

If quetzals could cry, they would have wept at the arrival of the Spaniards in Guatemala. Pedro de Alvarado and his soldiers brought with them new diseases that decimated the indigenous population. More than two-thirds of Guatemala's Indians perished. The survivors soon lost their lands to agricultural-export businesses responding to the increased European demand for cacao, from which cocoa is made. Indian groups were pushed progessively farther into the mountainous interior as they tried to preserve their culture built around the cultivation of corn.

In 1871 president Justo Rufino Barrios ordered the confiscation of church and Indian lands in order to establish the coffee industry. Overnight, thousands of Indians became landless, forced to pick coffee during the three-month harvest. In the early 1900s bananas began to compete with coffee. By 1912 the United States-based United Fruit Company gained considerable control over the Guatemalan economy and political system. It amassed over five hundred thousand acres of land, of which only fifteen percent was cultivated.

When president Jacobo Arbenz tried to expropriate all uncultivated land in 1952 to give to the landless peasants to raise food (offering to pay the United Fruit Company exactly the value they declared on the land for its taxes to the Guatemalan government), he was labeled "communist," and the CIA (Central Intelligence Agency) was enlisted to overthrow Guatemala's last freely elected civilian government. Although no troops were sent to Guatemala, the CIA paid American pilots to fly air raids for the rebels. On one such mission they hit a key military installation in Guatemala City, as well as an evangelical radio station. The United States-backed rebellion ousted the president and installed Colonel Carlos Castillo Armas, flown into the capital on the U.S. ambassador's plane.

The successive military governments that have ruled since 1954 have used U.S. military training and logistical support to reverse the reforms of 1944-54. The military rulers also became businessmen, amassing large estates while the plight of the poor grew worse.

Right-wing paramilitary groups and death squads were formed and began to terrorize and assassinate political opponents. Over one hundred thousand Guatemalan civilians have been killed or have "disappeared" (*desaparecido*) since 1954. Nearly forty percent of all "disappearances" (*desaparecidos*) in recent Central and South American history occurred in Guatemala.

—adapted from *The Other Side*, November 1987[1]

Even though Guatemala is rich in natural resources, 86 percent of the population lives in poverty and earns less than U.S. $216 a year. Small subsistence farmers occupy 16 percent of the country's arable land, while 72 percent of the land is used for export production (cotton, coffee, bananas, and beef). The traditional "Indian corn" has been replaced by nontraditional vegetables, such as Brussels sprouts and broccoli for export to the United States.[2]

Driven from their land, forced to live in military-controlled "model villages," reduced to sweated labor on large plantations, and threatened with death if they speak out against injustice, as many as 150,000 Guatemalans have fled to Mexico. Another one million have been driven from their homes to hide in the city slums or remote mountains of Guatemala. Over 100,000 children have lost one or both parents.[3]

If quetzals could cry. . . !

Meditation

Setting: Ask participants to place the photographs of family members that they have brought under a sign that says, "Disappeared."

Reflect: (Explain the background given in the introduction to this chapter. Then ask:) What feelings emerge when looking at someone loved who has "disappeared"? How would we react to the continued harassment, disappearance, and death of relatives and friends?

Scripture Passage: Exodus 3:7-9 (God sees the suffering of the Israelites). Paraphrase the same verses, applying them to Guatemala.

Support Human Rights in Guatemala: In recent years Guatemala has been the only Central American country in which no human rights group could even operate, so violent were the security forces and allied death squads. According to the Washington Office on Latin America, up to 50,000 people were killed in the 1980s alone.[4]

In 1984, family members of the "disappeared" organized into the Mutual Support Group (*Grupo de Apoyo Mutuo*), or GAM. Their purpose continues to be to help members find missing relatives. In March 1985, Army General Mejía Victores said publicly, "To seek the reappearance alive of those disappeared is a subversive act, and measures will be taken to deal with it." Leading members of GAM received death threats, then two of its officers were killed, one along with her younger brother and infant son.[5]

"This I Ask Ye" was written by a woman from the United States who has become an advocate for Guatemalans. After reading the poem, offer prayers of support. Discuss some ways to be supportive of Guatemalan human rights: 1) Ask some to do further research; 2) Check on advocacy through your church denomination or with local groups interested in Central America; 3) Obtain names from Amnesty International or the Guatemalan Human Rights Commission (see page 74 for addresses); 4) Call the media in your area or write a letter to the local newspaper, asking for coverage of the rapidly deteriorating human rights situation in Guatemala; 5) Write or call your national government leaders.

This I Ask Ye

Who have looked on cloth of Guatemala
And found it beautiful
in power: beyond description
Power to evoke a gentle life
life of land and water;
of Kulkulcán, and Chac;
of Ixchal and thick green jungle;
of yellow maize
and red and black;
of white bean flowers;
and of hammocks, lacy under blue sky.

Brown skin, soft and white smile flashing shy;
Think of her then, and her baby;
Weaver woman and son,
What future they?

This I ask ye:
Let thy feelings be known!
Write! Speak!
Weave thy life into life
   too for her
   and her people
   and her life.

Women of the Grupo de Apoyo Mutua (GAM) hold photographs of relatives who have been "disappeared."
Photo: Pat Goodvis

Please, I ask all fellow weavers:
Write or phone your congressman,
your senators, your president:
No Arms to Guatemala!
No support for a government that
slaughters its people, its gentle
effacing mountain weaver-people.
The Indios, who ask no more than
to be left alone on the bit of
poor jungle land that has been
left over for so long—and now
the government wants even that.

I charge you: write!
If you have ever loved cloth
        of Guatemala,
You owe the weaver a debt.
For the cloth came not of no-one.
It was a woman wove it.
It was a man dyed it.
It was a child got tangled
in the threads.

Love not only the cloth:
Love also the weaver.
And now we MUST,
We MUST
accept responsibility of love
and fight.
Sympathy is not enough:
Write!
                —Cheryl Kolander[6]

"Here in Guatemala, many times you see
something, but you don't say anything
because you don't want to die yet."
Archbishop Prospero Penados del Barrio
(quoted in Guatemala: Eternal Spring, Eternal Tyranny)

The Wounded Quetzal

Weariness,
rebellion,
pain,

determination,
longing,
dread.
Burdens gathered
on the long road through the Ixcán.
Suddenly,
upon returning:
tiny naked feet,
labored breathing,
a pleading look
toward an overcast sky.
Small trembling hand,
hopeless agony
of the small wounded quetzal,
overcome by death.
Little Indian child
constantly struggling against hunger.

Tiny timid face,
small obsidian eyes,
smiling and gentle.
Naked feet
creating paths
in the jungle.
Silent witness
to the agony of the quetzal
at last cuddled in the nest of your hands.

Little Indian child,
bearer of a thousand crosses
on your back
which was bent at birth.

Teacher of the earth,
of the forest,
of weeping,
and of laughter.

A hot coal sears my breast
and a cry I cannot stifle strikes at my heart.
It is the flapping of the quetzal
struggling to be free
from the blood-thirsty claws
of the condor
and the bald eagle.

Indian Guatemala,
in ever-present struggle
to break into flight
towards the broad horizon
of an ownerless land.

War cry!
Song of love
intoned by millions
of small Indian children
who are and will be born
holding hands
in unending games.
Fledgling quetzals
who test their flight
in the hands of the Brown Skinned Child*
who opens paths for us
there, from whence the birds of prey
have fled.

Fawns who climb the mountains,
who run like the offspring of gazelles,
over mountains filled with fragrances.

Run, run, Indian child,
run like a fawn toward the mountains;
there, where the quetzal makes
new and higher flights.

—Julia Esquivel (in exile)
from *Threatened with Resurrection*

*Jesus of Nazareth

27

Lament

"We scattered in the forests;
all our towns were taken; oh
my children were all slaughtered
by Tonatió." *

—from *The Annals of the Cakchiquel*
quoted in *The Wounded Quetzal*

* The Cakchiquel name for Pedro Alvarado.

The Root of Our Problem

The military took Rigoberta Menchú's father as a political prisoner in 1977, accusing him of being a communist and subversive because of his work in defense of Indian rights to their own land. He was set free, but later killed.

Our enemies were not only the landowners who lived near us, and above all not just the landowners who forced us to work and paid us little. It was not only now we were being killed; they had been killing us since we were children, through malnutrition, hunger, poverty. We started thinking about the roots of the problem and came to the conclusion that everything stemmed from the ownership of the land. The best land was not in our hands. It belonged to the big landowners. Every time they see that we have new land, they try to throw us off it or steal it from us in other ways.

—Rigoberta Menchú
from *I, Rigoberta Menchú.*

An Army Informant

You would be taking a bus from the capital to Chichi and everyone would be talking until you got to Tecpán. That was the signal: the bus would fall silent and the driver would become extremely nervous. No one would talk. All the passengers had to get off. With everyone lined up, the hooded man, accompanied by soldiers, would go down the line, looking at all the passengers. If the hooded man pointed someone out, the soldiers would grab him. If he went down the line without pointing anyone out, the passengers felt an indescribable relief, because they had just spent the past few minutes in hell.

—A resident of Chichicastenango
from *Guatemala: Eternal Spring, Eternal Tyranny*

False Accusation, Torture, Death

The government put about this image of us, of our family, as if we were monsters, as if we were some kind of foreigners, aliens. But my father was Quiché, he was no Cuban. The government called us communists and accused us of being a bad influence. So, in order to not expose the community to danger . . . we had to go away to different places. But my young brother had stayed there in the community.

Later the military took the brother, then tortured and killed him in front of people, including his mother and family, who were forced to watch.

I was watching the children. They were crying and terrified, clinging to their mothers. . . . During his speech, the captain kept saying his government was democratic and gave us everything. What more could we want? He said that the subversives brought foreign ideas, exotic ideas that would only lead us to torture, and he'd point to the bodies of the men. . . . They lined up the tortured and poured petrol on them; and then the soldiers set fire to each one of them. Many of them begged for mercy. . . .

After the slaughter: Well, the officer quickly gave the order for the squad to withdraw. They all fell back holding their weapons up and shouting slogans as if it were a celebration. They were happy! They roared with laughter and cried, "Long live the Fatherland! Long live Guatemala! Long live our President! Long live the army, long live (president) Lucas!"

—Rigoberta Menchú
from *I, Rigoberta Menchú*

Speaking Out

Alma América Garrido de Girón, a (nursery school) teacher, was abducted in Guatemala City on 14 January 1987 by unidentified men who forced her, in front of her 10-year-old daughter, into a car with darkened windows and no license plates. Her body was found three days later on the road between Escuintla and Antigua Guatemala, bearing signs of torture. According to local news reports, her father said at her funeral that he had not asked for justice from the authorities, as he suspected that those responsible were members of a government security agency.

—Amnesty International Report, April 1987

"Who in Your Family Has 'Disappeared'?"

"My father, Rigoberto Morales.
My brother, Máynor Morales.
My brother, Otto Raúl Morales.
My brother, Armando Roberto Morales.
My uncle, Moisés Morales.
My uncle, Salomón Morales.
My aunt, Lilián Morales.
My aunt, Elizabeth Morales.
My aunt, Sipriana Ramírez de Morales.
My cousin, Damaris Marleni Morales.
My cousin, María Victoria Morales.
My cousin, Héctor Manolo Morales.
My cousin, Noé Salomón Morales.
My cousin, Byron Moisés Morales.
My cousin, Abygail Morales.
My cousin, Claudia Morales."

—from *Guatemala: Eternal Spring, Eternal Tyranny*

Refugees / Chiapas

I cannot dispel these thoughts of you.
Across three thousand miles
you haunt me with cold hard facts.
You wait corralled high in the hills
of Chiapas*, remembering.
Is anyone left in the village
to weave the shrouds?

I saw you in Huehuetenango*
when you came down from the village
to market your cloth.

* *See glossary*

Fishers of Men

A song in Spanish sung in Latin America, but particularly in Guatemala, by the people when someone has been killed or "disappeared."

You have come to the water's edge,
not looking for the wise or the rich,
you only want me to follow you.

Chorus: Lord, you have looked into my eyes,
        smiling, you have spoken my name.
        In the sand I have left my boat,
        beside you I will search another sea.

You know well what I have done.
In my boat are neither gold or swords,
only nets and my work.

You need my hands,
my tiredness, so others can rest,
love that wishes to go on loving.

You, Fisherman of other waters,
eternal anxiety of souls who wait,
good friend who thus calls me.

           —C. Gabrarain, Spain

It was parrot-green, aqua, magenta, gold.
Is anyone left to learn from you
the art of the Mayan loom?

The wheel and the shuttle are still.
the brilliance that flowed like a song
from your highlands
has become a crimson stain
on the soul of the world.
Guatemala, mute with horror now,
survive to sing another day.

        —Stacie Smith-Rowe
          from *Sojourners*[7]

Sanctuary

Volunteers from Tucson brought seven Guatemalan refugees across the Mexican-U.S. border. They traveled on foot through the rugged Sonora desert, where vehicles picked them up and transported them to one of the eleven Tucson sanctuary churches. Church workers spent two days and two nights backpacking through the countryside with the family.

The family has lost seven family members to Guatemalan death squads, including their own nine- and ten-year-old daughters. "We knew we were under surveillance. We knew that leaving was the only alternative for people who are in danger of being murdered in our country. If we are sent back, there is no doubt we would be killed," said the father of the family.

Nena McDonald (one of sixteen indicted for helping the Sanctuary Movement) is a nurse and mother of two from Lubbock, Texas, who volunteered . . . with the Tucson Ecumenical Council. The press asked her why she did it. "If I walked down a street in Lubbock and saw a person lying in the street hurt, people would think something was wrong with me if I didn't help. What I have done for the refugees is no different. If people come here to drink from the well of kindness and we turn them away, we will have poisoned the well. Someday when we ourselves may need to drink from that same well, we will find it poisoned with floating bodies."

—Michael McConnell from *The Other Side*, March 1985[8]

Public identification could lead to deportation for refugees living in sanctuary.
Drawing: Gloria Claudia Ortiz.

FOUR
From Gods to God

A t the time of the conquest, the city of Tayasal flourished on the shores of Lake Petén. Hernando Cortez was the first Spaniard to visit this thriving city that is credited with over twenty-one places of worship, called *teocallis*, twelve of which would hold more than a thousand people each, with countless idols occupying prominent places.[1]

Unlike the Aztecs of Mexico and the Incas of Peru, the Mayas did not sacrifice human life. They were decidedly mystic and moved to the same *suave y dulce* (soft and sweet) rhythms as the surrounding hills and rounded cones of the volcanoes.[2] Even today those same hills, mountains, and volcanoes are sacred places. On the heights and in deep ravines are shrines where age-old rituals are still performed before the earth deity and the Ancestors (those from whom the people descended).[3]

No region in America appears to have furnished so many or such striking analogies to Christian ritual and symbolism as did the region of the Mayas. The cross, for example, signified many things to the Maya: the four winds of heaven, the four directions, and everlasting life. The Mayas also worshiped with elaborate ceremonies, incense, prayer, music, and images as symbols of deities long before "Christianity arrived on horse-back."[4]

Other rites similar to Roman Catholic religious practices were confession of sins, penitence, penance, and pilgrimages to holy shrines. Not only were Mayan rituals analogous to some Christian rituals, but some Mayan beliefs about the days of the Ancestors were similar to biblical events: a tradition of a flood, a confusion of tongues, and a dispersion of peoples.[5]

Soon Indians were adhering to a fusion of beliefs that combined elements of the Mayan and Roman Catholic ritual, and mixed the Mayan divinities with Catholic saints. "The Indian (array of gods) . . . frequently have both Mayan and Catholic names. . . . The main deities include a remote and inaccessible high god; subservient to him is a matrimonial couple, called variously Jesus and Mary, or the sun and the moon."[6]

Since the Catholic Church arrived in Guatemala in the sixteenth

century, it was willing to acquiesce in whatever the ruling class wanted. In the wake of the Second Vatican Council (1962-1965), the Church raised more questions about its own support of the established order. After the 1968 Medellin Bishops' Conference, thousands of priests and nuns changed the focus of their work to concentrate on the poorer communities. Their Bible study and Catholic Action groups led the poor majority to increased social and political awareness. Add to that the theme of Pope John Paul II's speech during his March 1983 visit to Guatemala: that Christianity demands "more than virulent anti-communism, and that failure to observe the most rudimentary demands of social justice (is) hardly more compatible with Christianity than atheistic Marxism."[7]

Late in the nineteenth century, Protestants were invited into Guatemala as part of the anti-Catholic policies of President Justo Rufino Barrios, but not until the 1970s did evangelicalism become a major social phenomenon. The growth of social and spiritual consciousness among the poor, the majority of whom are Indian, had often been rewarded with repression by the army. Desperate for community and for ways to cope with a repressive environment, many turned to evangelical sects. Pentecostal and Catholic charismatic communities, which tend to stress individual faith rather than social responsibility, also attracted the elite and the military, uneasy with the social justice orientation of many Catholic clergy and mainline Protestant groups.[8]

After the 1976 earthquake, the military backed Protestant fundamentalist sects in an effort to undermine any popular uprisings for human rights and equitable land distribution, principles fostered by Catholic and mainline Protestant groups.[9] By the early 1980s, nearly 6,800 Protestant congregations were divided among more than a hundred denominations.[10] By 1989 many in the Protestant community claimed their numbers to be as high as 35 percent of the population.

In spite of vehement anti-Catholic sentiment on the part of some fundamentalist sects, a new ecumenism is emerging. It is uniting Christians across denominational lines around "a common vision of the churches' mission to promote, not themselves, but rather God's reign of justice and peace."[11]

Meditation

Entering into "solidarity with the oppressed" means creating space in which the oppressed can both be heard and act on their own behalf. The voiceless need a voice. . . . The church must become a place where the only credential necessary to gain a hearing is a cry of pain. Once that cry is heard within the church, the church must become the loudspeaker through which the cry can be transmitted elsewhere.

—Robert McAfee Brown, from *Theology in a New Key*[12]

Scripture Passage: II Chronicles 7:14 ("If people humble themselves and pray").

Prayer: In Spanish-speaking countries, the Lord's Prayer is called the "Our Father" (el Padre Nuestro). Read antiphonally or in unison a contemporary "Our Father" composed by Salvadoran refugees in Mesa Grande, Honduras.

Our Father for Today

OUR FATHER, WHO ART IN HEAVEN,
you will that we your children
build a new earth of brotherhood
and sisterhood, and not a hell of
violence and death.

HOLY BE YOUR NAME, that in your
name, Lord, there be no abuse, no
oppression and no manipulation
of the conscience and liberty
of your children.

YOUR KINGDOM COME, not the
kingdom of fear, of power,
of money, of seeking peace by
means of war.

YOUR WILL BE DONE ON EARTH
AS IT IS IN HEAVEN, over
this land of ours and other
sister lands that changed their
songs of joy because of oppression
and the whine of shrapnel.

GIVE US THIS DAY OUR DAILY BREAD,
the bread of peace, Lord, so that
we can plant corn and beans,
watch them grow and share
them together as a family.

FORGIVE US OUR SINS AS WE FORGIVE
THOSE WHO SIN AGAINST US. May our
personal and national interests
be not the coin of our exchanges.
May our laments be changed into
songs of life, clenched fists into
open hands, cries of orphans
into smiles.

LEAD US NOT INTO TEMPTATION,
the temptation of conformism, of
doing nothing, the temptation to
refuse to work with you in the
search for justice and peace.

DELIVER US FROM EVIL of being
Cain to our brother, of being
arrogant, of believing ourselves
to be lords of life and death.

AMEN. That it be thus, Lord, as you will it,
according to your loving design. For yours is
the kingdom and the power and the glory.
You, Lord, are our ultimate salvation.
In you we place all our hope.

—from *Maryknoll* Magazine, May 1989[13]

Readings

The Land Is So Good

We were born learning how to plant: our survival depended on the
harvests. When my father would chop down a tree, he would ask the
world to forgive him because he knew that the tree had done nothing
to the man. And when he asked for forgiveness, he would say that
he was not doing it thoughtlessly, but out of necessity. My father would
pray to God, and ask him for forgiveness since, each year, he had to
wound the earth, but he would say that he did it only to survive. At
the same time, he would give thanks, because the land is so good, and
one knows it will not seek vengeance.

—from *Guatemala: Eternal Spring, Eternal Tyranny*

Prayers Before the Dance

The belief that the dance releases the deceased from a place of suffering, where they are bound with chains, provides probably the strongest motivation for an Aguacatec* man to perform the dance. Contrary to popular belief, he does not choose to dance because of his love for dancing, nor because of his fascination with the colorful costumes, nor because of a deep desire to be the center of attention. None of these reasons could entice him to make the financial sacrifice which he entails when he agrees to participate.

He is afraid of his deceased relatives who, to him, are not "dead" but instead are "imprisoned" or "bound." Through the complex ritual surrounding the dance, the dead are released. The *mam* (religious leader) perpetuates these fears by making audible prayers of imprecation, invoking evil upon the descendants of former dancers who refuse to propagate the custom.

> Father, punish those who do not want to dance.
> Come down upon them, Father!
> Come down upon them!
> Lend me an owl, Father!
> Lend us an owl for a little while!
> Lend us a night hawk!
> Lend us a mountain cat to frighten them, Father!
> Send the dark shadow of the wind upon them. . . .
> Oh, that they might go to the place of suffering.

When the dead return to the land of the living, having been released through the costumed dance, "they walk in death wherever they walked in life. That is why we put shoes in the grave with our dead," volunteered one Aguacatec.

> Father, everything is fine now.
> Your children have come before you.
> Come out of the place of the dead.
> Come out of jail.
> Come out from under the stocks.
> Come out.
> Come out to the light of day,
> Because your costumes (dancers) are coming now.
> Your costumes are coming.
> Come out a little while into the sunshine.

—from *Cognitive Studies of Southern Mesoamerica*

*The Aguacatec are one of the Mayan tribes.

Some Indian Beliefs and Practices

Indians growing tired on a trail will cut a branch from a tree and switch their legs with it to acquire sufficient strength from the deity in the tree to continue.

When approaching a hot spring, they gather bundles of sticks to place beside it for the god who boils water so the god will not heat the Indians' blood and cause a fever.

In the highlands, some will remove a sandal from the right foot to leave weariness behind.

An eclipse, they believe, is caused when the sun and moon fight, which may bring the end of the world. Entire village populations beat on pots, pans, drums, and shoot off fireworks to distract the sun and moon, thereby driving away the enveloping shadow.

When an owl sings, an Indian dies.

Religious leaders turn caskets around and around at the gravesite to fool the devil and give the spirit the right direction toward heaven.

Twin ears of corn contain the "spirit of the corn," an assurance of a good crop next season. One is kept for seed, the other is placed as a thank offering to the household saint (and must be guarded from theft).

—from *Four Keys to Guatemala*

The Black Christ of Esquipulas

Indians, terrified by the cruelty of the Spaniards, believed that all white people were evil and that Christ could not be a kind and charitable god if he were white. Priests commissioned Quirio Catao in 1594 to make an image of Christ from balsam wood whose dark color resembles the complexion of the Indian. After centuries of incense and candle smoke, the statue has blackened completely.

—from *Four Keys to Guatemala*

Broken Bone Healing Ritual Prayer

The Ixil Maya of the Guatemalan highlands possess a rich oral poetic genre that finds its fullest expression in such formal situations as requesting a bride and ushering in a new year. In contrast to most of our Western poetic forms in which lines of verse conform to rhythmic patterns, Ixil poetry depends heavily on units of similar meanings. This is most evident in parallelism; for example, couplets with the second line directly below the first.

This ritual prayer is used to unlock the supernatural powers on the petitioner's behalf. The majority of illnesses, from spider bites to broken bones, are attributed to spirit world phenomena. Mam Te'c Cham, the healer who prayed the following prayer, suspects that the man's broken bone is the result of a malevolent spell cast on his client.

Jesus Mary Joseph,
Jesus Mary Christ;
  my God the buried one,
  my God the bruised one.
So here's to you good bone,
        good vein;
      . . . bone,
      . . . vein;
      male bone,
      male vein;
so how could your head have turned;
how could your being   have turned?
What have you done?
  Were you hurt;
  were you shaken?
And who has made you cry;
    who has called for you?
. . . .
(*Healer blows and rubs on broken area.*)
You will go in straight;
you will go in united.
So you will go in right;
    you will go in a wrap/bandage.
. . . .
So I will make you go straight.
God the bruised one;
God the buried one.
Since I am your lady;
    I am your lord.
  I will make you go in right;
  I will make you a (whole) bone.
. . . .
You will go in right;
you will go in.
(*Healer blows and wraps broken area with a rag.*)

      —Mam Te'c Cham
        from *Ritual Rhetoric from Cotzal*

Religion and Culture

By accepting the Catholic religion, we didn't accept a condition, or abandon our culture. It was more like another way of expressing ourselves. . . . We believe we have ancestors, and that these ancestors are important because they're good people who obeyed the laws of our people. The Bible talks about (ancestors) too. So it is not something unfamiliar to us.

—Rigoberta Menchú, from *I, Rigoberta Menchú*

Christians or Communists?

In 1982, Colonel Roberto Mata Gálvez, who became President Cerezo's Presidential Chief of Staff, said, "We (the army) make no distinction between the Catholic Church and communist subversion."

—from *Guatemala: Eternal Spring, Eternal Tyranny*

Catholics or Protestants?

Protestantism did not exist in Guatemala until 1882. Today, as much as thirty-five percent of the population is Protestant. In Guatemala City alone there are some five hundred Protestant churches. The rise of Protestantism in Guatemala had little to do with the fact that General Rios Montt, who became president in 1982, was Protestant. Even after his overthrow, his Evangelical "Church of the Word" continued to grow so rapidly that in 1985 it moved to a former roller skating rink.

The growth of Protestantism, in general terms, is partly due to its hands-on approach. "Since there is a permanent ambience of incertitude in Guatemala," one analyst explained, "people look for something to participate in."

The Protestant Church appealed to the *ladinos*, those who chose to become "Westernized." In recent decades the Roman Catholic Church began to identify with the powerless of Guatemala instead of the powerful, which resulted in its persecution and a mass exodus of many of its people. Catholic leaders were considered subversive for having "organized" people to work for justice. In the late 1970s and early 1980s, hundreds of catechists* were killed and thousands of Catholics either converted to Protestantism or no longer practiced their religion.

As one Guatemalan explained:

> Back in 1975 and 1976 there were only four or five families in town who were Protestants. They weren't looked upon well by Indians, who would say that they were getting 'mixed up in gringo things.' By 1978 and 1979, however, people were realizing that the Protestants were much safer, and that was when Catholic Action declined and the Protestants became much more numerous. In 1978, people began asking for letters of recommendation from a local Protestant institute, to prove that they had worked there, so the army wouldn't bother them. One of my friends told me that he had converted to Protestantism so that the army wouldn't come to kill him and he could go to the capital to sell his *huipiles.***

—quote from *Guatemala: Eternal Spring, Eternal Tyranny*

* Catholic laypersons who lead Bible studies and organize people for community social action. ** See glossary

Catholics/Protestants Working Together

We spent some time visiting an evangelical church in a rural area whose members are drawn from the indigenous population. . . . This Protestant community works closely with the local Catholic parish. Catholics and Protestants study the Bible together and work together for the good of the community.

The wife of the pastor, herself a religious instructor, explained that this ecumenical perspective began in 1976 when the two communities began to cooperate after a devastating earthquake virtually leveled their town. They drew closer together during the violent massacres of Indians in the early 1980s. "We discovered there is no difference between Catholics and Evangelicals in the Bible," she said. "All Christians belong to the one Body of Christ."

This evangelical community sponsors many projects, such as weaving cooperatives which help provide income for more than 500 widows and 1200 orphans in the region. They have also helped link together fifteen families who farm a plot of land together and share its produce.

Here the Bible was the essential charter for a divine mandate of liberation of society from oppression, not only of the rich against the poor, but also the domination of men over women.

—Rosemary Radford Ruether
from *Christianity and Crisis,* July 10, 1989[14]

Faith and Poverty

I know that no-one can take my Christian faith away from me. Not the government, nor fear, nor weapons. And this is what I have to teach my people: that together we can build the people's Church, a true Church. Not just a hierarchy, or a building, but a real change inside people. I chose this as my contribution to the people's war. I am convinced that the people, the masses, are the only ones capable of transforming society. It's not just another theory. I chose to stay in the city among the people, instead of choosing to take up arms.

. . . That is my cause. . . . It wasn't born out of something good, it was born out of wretchedness and bitterness. It has been radicalized by the poverty in which my people live. It has been radicalized by the malnutrition which I, as an Indian, have seen and experienced. And by the exploitation and discrimination which I've felt in the flesh. And by the oppression which prevents us performing our ceremonies, and shows no respect for our way of life, the way we are.

—Rigoberta Menchú
from *I, Rigoberta Menchú*

Statement of Beliefs

We (*Rigoberta Menchú and others*) began studying more deeply and, well, we came to a conclusion. That being a Christian means thinking of our [brothers and sisters] around us, and that every one of our Indian race has the right to eat. This reflects what God said, that on this earth we have a right to what we need. The Bible was our principal text for study as Christians and it showed us what the role of a Christian is. . . .

It is not God's will that we should live in suffering, that God did not give us that destiny, but that [people] on earth have imposed this suffering, poverty, misery and discrimination on us. . . . Our reality teaches us that, as Christians, we must create a Church of the poor, that we don't need a Church imposed from outside which knows nothing of hunger. . . .

We have understood that being a Christian means refusing to accept all the injustices which are committed against our people, refusing to accept the discrimination committed against a humble people who barely know what eating meat is but who are treated worse than horses. . . .

Unless a religion springs from within the people, it is a weapon of the system. . . .

We feel it is the duty of Christians to create the kingdom of God on Earth among our [brothers and sisters]. . . .

We don't need a king in a palace but a brother who lives with us. We don't need a leader to show us where God is, to say whether he exists or not, because, through our own conception of God, we know there is a God and that, as the father of us all, he does not wish even one of his children to die, or be unhappy, or have no joy in life.

—Rigoberta Menchú, from *I, Rigoberta Menchú*

Base Community

A sixteen-year-old non-Christian with the very Christian name of Maria becomes involved in a "base community," one of thousands of such groups all over the continent that meets for prayer, Bible study, and social action, with a heavy emphasis on the "social action" so that their lives are always in danger. After a time, Maria wants to be baptized and confirmed. But the priest demurs. He thinks it might be better to wait a little longer for Maria to join the church, until she has matured more fully. "I'm not sure," says the priest, "that Maria is yet ready to die for her faith."

By her eighteenth birthday, Maria has been baptized and confirmed and has died for her faith.

—Robert McAfee Brown, from *Unexpected News*

FIVE
A Living Tapestry:
Stories and Interviews

A friend who worked for several years in Bolivia moved to Guatemala. "My first impression," she said, "was the difference between Bolivian and Guatemalan woven articles. The Bolivians use dull, dark colors, often with no design. In Guatemala, even though the background of a tapestry often is black, a riot of colors runs through the cloth, creating exotic patterns, even pictures."

A woman's hand-woven *huipil*, her blouse, reveals where she lives, her ethnic background, and her marital status, as well as the ancient beliefs of the Mayas. A pioneer collector and documentor of Guatemalan textiles, Lily de Jongh Osborne, says, "The Indians of Guatemala have never had to wait for trees to be turned into paper, or paper into books. Their textiles were their books and each one wrote (her) own."[1]

No matter how skilled the persons who weave, they never make a piece of cloth perfect. Even the finest textiles woven for the highest dignitaries or for the most sacred ceremonies will have a small patch left undecorated or made with unmatched threads. Their reasoning: only the gods and their works are perfect. Who would dare to equal them?[2]

Even though eighty percent of the rural Indian people of Guatemala are illiterate,[3] they understand the importance of "telling their story" by oral tradition or woven into cloth. Such stories depict life with all of its flaws. And such stories woven in cloth reveal the wearer's tribal identity. That is reason enough to hide oneself in Western dress rather than to be a target for death squads intent on wiping out the stories of those involved in the struggle for human rights.

Meditation

Four little words, "Once upon a time," can pique the interest of children and adults alike. No wonder Jesus often spoke in parables. He knew that stories cement the truth in people's minds much better than sermons laced with facts and figures. We are drawn to the gospel more easily when it comes in story form.

*Guatemalan refugees in Mexico
have developed artisan cooperatives to preserve traditional
weaving and other arts.*
Photo: Derrill Bazzy

Hymn: "Tell Me the Stories of Jesus."

Scripture Passage: Luke 10:29-38 (The Good Samaritan).

Reflect: Put the story of the Good Samaritan in modern context. Replace the man who was robbed and beaten with the people of Guatemala. Reread the story, asking such questions as:
- Who are the robbers, those who strip possessions and beat the innocent?
- Who are the high, religious authorities who ignore the suffering and injustice in Guatemala?
- What other groups of people and organizations deny that anything is wrong in that country?
- Who are the Samaritans?
- How do they respond to the situation?
- What is our response?

Prayer:

Open my eyes, that I may see
   those who have been beaten, robbed
   and left for dead
   in Guatemala
   and other parts of God's world.

Open my ears, that I may hear
   cries of injustice, anger,
   and pain
   as people pour out stories
   of torture and death.

Open my mouth, that I may spread
   the truth, without fear,
   to others who refuse
   to believe the complicity
   we all share.

Open my heart, illumine me,
   Spirit Divine.

Readings

Buying Land We Already Own

During the administration of President Barrillas (1885-1892), the govern-ment took large areas of land from the Indians and gave them to *ladinos**
for coffee raising. One day hundreds of Indians from Nahualá, in full
tribal costume, arrived before the Palace in Guatemala City. Alarmed,
the President ordered that only the Nahualá's *Alcalde** and Municipal
Secretary be permitted to enter. The Indians refused; they had come
as one body, they would be admitted as one body.

Admitted they were. When they entered the reception hall, they
fell on their knees in rows, foreheads to the floor. One remained erect,
"a tall, well-dressed Indian of severe yet serene countenance." And
when the President commanded that the others rise, this spokesman
said, "I will not order my companions to rise, señor Presidente, until
you have given us justice, for it is justice we have come to ask. . . .

"You have ordered us to leave our lands so that coffee can be sown
there. You have done us an injustice. In exchange you have offered
us 600 *caballerias** of land on the coast. What do we want of land
on the coast? Our brothers, our women, our children will die there.
. . . You ask us to leave the land where our grandfathers and fathers
were born, where we were born, where our sons were born. . . . Why
have you committed this injustice? Is it because we do not know how
to grow coffee? You know very well we know how to grow coffee,
señor presidente. Are we not the ones who sow the coffee on the
*fincas,** wash it, harvest it?. . .

"But we do not wish to grow coffee on our lands. We want them
only for our corn, our animals, our wood. And we want these lands
where our grandfathers and fathers worked. Why should we leave them?

"These lands have always been ours and furthermore we have paid
for them three times. . . . We paid for them in the time of President
Carrera (1838-1865); here are our titles to them. We bought them
the second time from President Cerna (1866-1870). . . . And we bought
them for the third time from President Barrios" (1871-1885).

With each statement, he opened his bag and drew out the proper
titles, placing them before the President.

"And now, do you wish that we buy them from you also? Very well.
We have brought the money. How much do you want for our own
lands, *señor Presidente?*"

President Barrillas had no reply except to order in the presence
of the Indians that not an inch of Nahualá lands should ever be taken
from them.

—from *Four Keys to Guatemala*

* See glossary

48

Want To Buy a Machete?

A small voice speaking perfect English (said), "Lady, want to buy a machete?"

I looked down to see the high-powered salesman. He was no more than two-and-a-half feet tall; his blue denim pants and red checked shirt had been mended often. . . .

"What is your name, little man?"

"John," he said.

"It can't be John. You are either Spanish or Indian."

"I am Indian, lady, and my name is John. I speak English; I do not speak Spanish at all."

"Where did you learn English?" I asked.

"In school. They teach us English so we can talk to people like you. Then we can sell you what we make."

. . . I wondered how long visitors would see what we saw at Chichicastenango. The flying pole, pagan rites with candles and petals, the dances which tell history in rythmic form—they are passing from the heartfelt to the picturesque and into the theatrical. I have seen how Waikiki has gone into Coney Island with fake grass huts and debased hula dancing. Here at Chichi youngsters learn English in school so that they can sell stuff to tourists to get the "fast buck" mentality. They will grow up [with] an entirely different outlook from their parents.

—Sister Mary Corde
  Lorang
  adapted from *Footloose Scientist in Maya America*

49

If They Could Have One Wish

Josefa, her husband, and six children lived in a small town in the mountains of Guatemala. Life was hard, but they managed to keep tortillas on the table. Then one day in 1984, military troops swept through the town, reportedly looking for "subversives." Josefa was left a widow, as were 129 other women of the town.

How do you feed six small children when the family's breadwinner is permanently removed? Josefa, though unschooled, sensed the fact that most women in Guatemala lose half of their children to curable diseases, brought on by malnutrition, before the children are five. Hardly a week goes by in her life that some neighbor or friend doesn't bury an *angelito* (little angel). Now without a husband, how could Josefa feed her children and keep them healthy?

She faced her bleak existence with a stoicism common to her Indian heritage. Then one day a widowed friend rushed over with the news that someone from an organization called PEACE for Guatemala** (Program for Emergency Assistance, Cooperation, and Education) would be at their church that evening.

"Our pastor says that the people from PEACE are beginning a project for our town. They will help us buy seed corn to plant in our *milpas** so we can feed our children," she said, her face filled with the most animation and hope since she became a widow.

That same hope has extended to Elena. She lives in the capital city of Guatemala with her husband and three children. Both she and her husband have to work in order to meet the expenses of living in a large city. The only job she could find was in a textile factory, a two-hour bus ride each way.

At first glance, Elena would seem to be better off than Josefa, but Elena's problem is fear for her children's safety. She and her husband belong to a labor union and are involved in the labor movement of Guatemala. Recently, another labor leader's son was shot while walking with his father, and was subsequently paralyzed. Why should innocent children be hurt, even killed, just because their parents are organizing for better working conditions and a living wage?

Elena found hope in a women's group that is helping her deal with problems her family faces. Funded by PEACE, the group includes women whose husbands are actively seeking to resolve the struggle within Guatemala. The group discusses solutions to their problems and ways in which, as women, they can become more involved in the struggle for economic justice. Elena still fears for her family's safety, but she finds hope in the fact that many others join with her: agriculture workers, health workers, teachers, and labor leaders.

Josefa lives in a small town in the mountains; Elena lives in cosmopolitan Guatemala City, but Reginaldo is exiled in southern Mexico. He longs to return safely to the land his people have farmed for hundreds and hundreds of years in Guatemala. He, like Josefa and Elena, has found encouragement from PEACE. The organization is helping Mayan farmers like Reginaldo to restore life and hope by providing programs in both Guatemala and Mexico where many Indians still live in exile because they are too frightened to return to the lands of their ancestry.

Two of Reginaldo's sons were killed by the military, so he fled with his wife and other members of their community across the border into southern Mexico. Since their arrival in 1981 they have tried to reestablish their community and do the kind of farming they did in Guatemala. PEACE has helped them to buy land and build permanent homes. The organization helped the exiles to plant corn, beans, and other vegetables, as well as to raise turkeys for export and rabbits for their own use. Reginaldo's wife was encouraged to join others in developing the beautiful Mayan crafts that are in danger of being lost forever as people's lives and culture are disrupted and threatened.

PEACE for Guatemala is bringing hope to the Josefas, Elenas, and Reginaldos of that country. The group is creating awareness and support in the United States and Canada, which generates help for the people of Guatemala. PEACE was launched in 1983 by forty-one different human rights and church organizations. Among the founding sponsors are representatives of Oxfam America, the Presbyterian Church (U.S.A.), Lutheran World Relief, Clergy and Laity Concerned, the American Friends Service Committee, and the Mennonite Central Committee. Cooperating with church and other groups within Guatemala, but never with the Guatemalan government, this nondenominational, nonpartisan organization fulfills needs to overcome unprecedented human suffering there.

Josefa, Elena, Reginaldo, and thousands of other Guatemalans live with the fear that sudden, violent death can visit them at any time and any place in their country. If they could have one wish, it would be that we in the United States and Canada would know the truth and would commit ourselves to help end the terror, deprivation, and devastation they face every day.

Will reading their stories make a difference?

—adapted from a PEACE newsletter

** For further information, see page 74. * See glossary.

Me Llamo Mateo: A Peasant's Lament

Me llamo Mateo. My name is Mateo. I come from the South Coast, where my father has a little plot of land. It was not enough to sustain our family; so ever since I can remember I worked in the fields during the harvest to try to bring in a little money.

I always dreamed of owning my own land, but that seemed impossible. Then I heard the army was opening up a housing development in the interior, a "development pole" they called it. They were resettling people from the war zones there but also making land available to others to settle. Some people from my village moved there, and they sent back word that it was true.

So two-and-a-half years ago, I left my family and moved with my wife Marta to this little village, San Miguel. Well, it was hardly a village, just a few roads and plots of land waiting to be cleared. . . .

I was happy to get my little plot of land. I worked hard to clear the jungle, burning and cutting the underbrush with my machete. In a little time, Marta and I built our home. It's not much—just one room with a dirt floor—but it's ours, and we worked hard to make it a home. I cleared the land, and we planted fruit trees, bananas, pineapples, and even some flowers. . . . I dug a well so that Marta would not have to walk a kilometer to the river to get water.

Here our two children were born. Little Blanca—she is only a few months old and sleeps much of the time in the hammock in the shade. Mateocito—little Mateo—he is almost three. He loves to work with me in the garden and pull the weeds. . . . Someday he will work with me in the fields.

When I came here, there was nothing, just the jungle. We worked hard to clear the land and get our first crops planted, and we were so proud the first time we could sell some of our crops. It was bad here in '82 when the army and guerrillas fought, but things had gotten calmer. . . .

Now this zone is heating up. Some of my neighbors say it will be worse this year than in '82; others say no. Who knows? But I don't want to see happen to my children what happened in La Trinidad.

It's a little village only a kilometer from here. One day in '82 the army came and surrounded the village. They accused the people of being subversives and began to threaten them and question them about the guerrillas. Then they began to kill them, sometimes tossing the littlest children into the air to see who could shoot them before they hit the ground or catch them on the ends of their bayonets. They killed everyone; it was a massacre.

And now the zone is hot again. Three weeks ago the guerrillas came and talked for three hours. . . . If we work with them, the army kills us. If we work with the army, the guerrillas bother us. And it's families that suffer. We just want to live *tranquilo,* in peace.

After the guerrillas left, the army found out and came in helicopters and bombed the village. . . . So now we are leaving our land and little house. It hurts me to have to leave this behind. We don't want to go, but it is not safe here.

We'll go back to my father's land, and I can work in the fields there. Perhaps I can get another job spraying pesticides as I did before. I don't want to go back to the coast—I'm always sick there, but what can I do?. . .

I cried when I shut the windows and closed the door the last time. My wife called for me to come, but I didn't want to. . . . I don't want to have to choose between my children and my land—they are both important. But I don't want to see happen to my children what happened to the children in La Trinidad.

—a narrative created from the accounts of several people, by Daniel Spencer
Adapted from *The Other Side*, November 1987[4]

Helping Through UNICEF

Intelligent, cultured, well-educated, and active in professional circles, Lucy Ayala nevertheless is much involved in addressing critical conditions born out of the struggle for justice in Guatemala.

A public accountant, a university professor of economy, two directors of schools, a doctor, lawyer, auditor, dress designer, manager of a medical laboratory, a director and owner of a business school, and an executive-secretary of a bank—all are women of Guatemala. Lucy Ayala, one of their colleagues, is the administrative assistant of the United Nations office for UNICEF in Central America.

Mrs. Ayala had just been named president of the Soroptimist Clubs of Guatemala. Gracing the coffee table in her well-furnished living room were two beautiful bouquets of flowers in honor of the occasion.

Lucy and her husband, Alfonso, were born in Guatemala City. Both studied in the United States for a few years. He became a pilot and later worked for Pan American Airlines in Guatemala City. He now sells real estate and finds time to do oil paintings of Guatemalan scenes, several of which hang on the walls of their home.

The Ayalas have two sons. Virgilio, the youngest, is on the board of directors of an association concerned with the construction of inexpensive but durable buildings in earthquake zones. Their older son, Alfonso, Jr., a medical doctor, has opted against a lucrative practice in Guatemala City. He chose instead to do public health work in Honduras, holding clinics for the poor and helping the communities to organize. He cooperated for a while with a group that builds low-cost housing and helps to bring water to villages. Now Alfonso, Jr., is considering an assignment to Belize, with conditions just as primitive.

Just as Alfonso is finding a way to address injustice and poverty in Central America, his mother finds fulfillment in her job at UNICEF and as a leader of Soroptimists. Together these two organizations are working to improve the living conditions in Mezquital, a squatter community near Guatemala City.

"People invaded part of a large *finca*, a ranch, on three different occasions," said Lucy Ayala. "Finally President Cerezo's wife asked that the poor be allowed to stay. Now the government must pay the owner for the land. UNICEF has an urban program to put in water and sanitation for the 25,000 people who have moved into the area."

Mrs. Ayala, through UNICEF, plays a part in such development projects as sewage treatment, terracing land, and reforestation. She spoke with great animation about developing community orchards, gardens, and schools, as well as getting all of the children vaccinated.

In spite of her heavy responsibilities, she is finding time to pursue a doctorate in art history at the Francisco Marroquín University. "I just hope all my grandchildren can come to my graduation," she said, smiling.

—Interview by the author, Guatemala City, July 1989

An Honor and a Cross

Fifteen-year-old Concepción Ramírez had just received the highest honor ever bestowed on a Tzutujil Indian. For weeks the suspense had been growing. The Guatemalan government was searching for the most beautiful girl among the many different Indian tribes.

At first Concepción, better known as Chonita by her family and friends, refused to take seriously the idea that she should enter the competition. Many of her friends in Santiago Atitlán insisted that she should allow her name to be included on the growing list of contenders. "You are more beautiful than any other girl we know," they said.

Chonita demurred. Her father would probably disapprove of such a "worldly" activity as a beauty contest. He was the pastor of a large evangelical church and a strict, although loving, father. He was especially protective of Chonita.

"Ask him," her friends pleaded. "We'll go with you and ask him ourselves." Though she thought the whole idea useless, she took her friends home with her. When they arrived, they found several prominent leaders of the town discussing their choice of the most beautiful Tzutujil Indian girl—Chonita. Her father had already given his approval for her to enter the contest.

If Chonita was surprised to receive her father's approval, she could hardly believe the outcome of the competition. She looked down the line of girls in their typical Tzutujil dress. Each wore a wrap-around skirt, a hand-woven huipil, and a red head covering rolled and twisted into a halo. Suddenly the colors blurred through Chonita's tears as she realized that the other contestants were surrounding her with congratulations. She was chosen as the most beautiful Tzutujil Indian to compete against the winners of each of the other twenty-one Indian groups.

For a fifteen-year-old Indian girl to cross Lake Atitlán in 1974 and travel to Guatemala City was exciting. For that same girl to stand in front of the president of her country was almost more than Chonita could imagine. Yet there she stood with twenty-one other Indian girls in their distinctive dress.

The president walked by each girl, looking at her face and costume. Once in a while he would pause for a longer inspection. He seemed to walk right by Chonita with only a glance, but she smiled at him in spite of her thumping heart. He retraced his steps, looking at each

girl before returning to the podium. After checking documents, he asked that Concepción Ramírez step forward. Chonita almost fainted.

"I hereby name you, Concepción Ramírez of the Tzutujils, the most beautiful young woman of all twenty-two Indian tribes. You will have the honor of representing all of the Indians of Guatemala by having your likeness stamped on the new twenty-five-cent coin soon to be minted."

For the next several months Chonita's life was a whirlwind of new experiences. She sat for photographs and portrait paintings. She appeared on television and met many important people, but she longed to be with her own people—especially with one young man.

Chonita married. Life in Santiago Atitlán was peaceful—until 1980. The military began to harass the Indian citizens, suspicious that some in the town were "guerrillas." Chonita saw little reason to worry. She still basked in the honor the government had given her and her people.

Each day her father would row his two grandsons across the lake to work in the family's cornfields. He returned to town to supervise the construction of their new church building. One evening when he crossed the lake to pick up his grandsons, some men with guns ordered him out of the boat. He was in his work clothes, so was not carrying his identification document. The men shot him.

The two boys found their grandfather's body near the boat. When they arrived on the opposite side of the lake, they found the whole town in tears and terror. Twenty-one other people had also been massacred that same day.

Today Chonita lives in poverty. Her husband, who lives in fear, has turned to alcohol. Her children often are hungry. Chonita, once the most beautiful Indian of Guatemala, whose face still graces the twenty-five-cent coin, seldom has two *quetzales** to call her own.

—A story based on fact

* Guatemalan coin made up of one hundred *centavos* (cents).

SIX
Threads of the Tapestry

Children, wherever you may be, do not abandon the crafts taught to you by Ixpiyacoc, because they are the crafts passed to you by our Ancestors. If you forget them, you will be betraying your lineage.

—Diego Reinoso, from *Popol Vuh*
quoted in *The Wounded Quetzal*

The Huipil*

This masterpiece of fine, handcrafted embroidery, brilliant with every color of the spectrum, is fashioned to project a concept of the cosmos that has been held by all Maya peoples for more than two thousand years. The opening for the head in the center of the *huipil* is representative of the sun, the greatest of deities, and its rays are formed by the ribbons around the opening. The rosettes of ribbon embroidered on the chest, the back, and the shoulder are the four cardinal points of the compass, symbolic of the four dimensions of the Maya universe. . . . The stripes of the *huipil* are the golden cornfields, and the diamonds represent kernels of maize, the food that has nourished the Maya since the time of the First People. The zigzag patterns are the sacred mountains that surround the villages where the deities and the Ancestors have dwelt since time immemorial.

—Kenneth Pearce
from *The View from the Top of the Mountain*

* Hand-woven blouse

Woven throughout the tapestry of life in Guatemala are the dark threads of injustice, poverty, and suffering. In spite of that somber background, the bright colors of love of family, tasty but simple foods, humor, and a mystical communion with God and God's creation brighten and give strength for the day and hope for the future.

58

"The Mothers are the teachers of the next generations. They imprint our spirits with hope and guarantee the Mayan traditions" (Quote from Ayuda "Women of Courage" calendar).
Photo: Pat Goodvis

Meditation

The age-old craft of weaving occupies deft fingers in Guatemala as the women create textiles in brilliant colors. The symbolic designs spring out of dark backgrounds and often picture the sacred ceiba tree or the quetzal. A backward-looking coyote symbolizes the animals that helped the Mayan gods discover corn, from which the four original men were made (see page 16). The zigzag line has several meanings: mountains, lightning, or the steep temple steps.

The most frequently used colors in Guatemalan Indian textiles are the colors of corn: yellow, red, white, and black.[1] What seems to be an attempt to brighten a drab, almost hopeless existence could also be an expression of eternal hope for a better tomorrow.

Weavers of fine cloth have used their talents throughout cultures and centuries. The Bible cites examples of skilled designers and their works of woven art.

Scripture Passages: Exodus 35:35 (Ability to weave).
Exodus 28:31-36 (Weaving a robe for Aaron).
John 19:23b (Jesus' tunic without seams).

Symbolic Action: Give each person different colored ribbons or strands of yarn. As a prayer activity, place them one at a time on a table, creating a simple pattern. For each ribbon or strand, make a prayerful request for the people and country of Guatemala, based on the symbolism of the color used.

Red: fire, warmth, life
Blue: sky, nobility
Yellow: sorrow, death

Green: eternal life, God
Purple: ceremonial

End the meditation on a note of hope, perhaps by reading:

Tapestry of Hope

Through the colorless life
tinged with black fear and death,
runs a rainbow of love:
God's promise divine.

Through the thunder of war
sewn with hunger and pain,
runs a ribbon of green:
God's undying hope.

Through the dark days and nights
washed with worry and tears,
runs a thread of new life:
God's redeeming love.

Readings

WEAVING

Textiles and Prayer

Long ago a textile was begun with prayer. It would require months to weave and would be worn and used for years with all the pride of ownership and craftsmanship. Something of the owner's own spirit was thought to be woven in it. Even today personal pieces are parted with reluctantly, kissed and fondled in farewell, and sometimes the man, if the textile is part of his woman's costume, will beat it to make sure that no part of her spirit remains to go with the purchaser.

—Vera Kelsey and Lilly de Jongh Osborne
from *Four Keys to Guatemala*

Textiles and the Military

Each of the twenty-two Indian tribes wears distinctive dress. If a woman wears her head-covering rolled and twisted into a red halo, she is from Santiago Atitlán and nowhere else.

The military studies *huipil* designs to identify members of villages where they suspect anti-government or pro-Indian groups to be located. Many Indians have felt forced to abandon the wearing of their *traje típico* (typical clothing).

I can't get accustomed to taking off my dress. I can't adjust to putting on other clothes. I can only wear other clothes for an hour or two.

I can't leave my dress, it's part of me. Without my dress I don't feel calm inside, I feel like I'm missing something, something from me. . . .

—A Mayan weaver quoted in *The Wounded Quetzal:
Women and Weaving in Guatemala*

Textiles and the Person

What hurts Indians most is that our costumes are considered beautiful, but it's as if the person wearing it didn't exist.

—Rigoberta Menchú
from *I, Rigoberta Menchú*

Indian Tapestry

When I go up to the HOUSE OF THE OLD WEAVER,
I watch in admiration
at what comes forth from her mind:
a thousand designs being created
and not a single model from which to copy
the marvelous cloth
with which she will dress
the companion of the True and Faithful One.

Men always ask me
to give the name of the label,
to specify the maker of the design.
But the Weaver cannot be pinned down
by designs,
nor patterns.
All of her weavings are originals,
there are no repeated patterns.
Her mind is beyond all foresight.
Her able hands do not accept
patterns nor models.
Whatever comes forth, comes forth,
but she who is will make it.

The colors of her threads
are firm:
blood,
sweat,
perseverance,
tears,
struggle,
and hope.
Colors that do not fade
with time.

The children of the children
of our children
will recognize the seal
of the Old Weaver.
Maybe then it will receive a name.

Derrill Bazzy

But as a model,
it can never again
be repeated.

Each morning I have seen how her fingers
choose the threads
one by one.
Her loom makes no noise
and men give it no importance,
none-the-less,
the design
that emerges from Her Mind
hour after hour
will appear in the thread of many colors,
in figures and symbols
which no one, ever again,
will be able to erase
or un-do.

—Julia Esquivel (in exile), from *Threatened with Resurrection*

FOOD

Corn, the Essence of Life

Maize is undeniably the most important staple in Mesoamerica.* It produces the greatest share of food from local domesticates, and occupies a symbolic and sacred status among many Indian groups. The Indians classify the different types grown at different altitudes and temperatures, and can answer the following questions about the kind being planted:

May this type of maize be planted in the same hole with beans? May it be stored for a long period of time or does it have poor resistance to disease, insects and rot? Does this type bring the highest price if one has to sell? Is it hard to shell? Does it have a smooth husk that is good for wrapping *tamalitos* or is it rough and non-flexible, hence worthless for this use?. . . Is the stalk long and thick and strong for use in building corrals and houses? What kind of tortillas does it make— one that remains soft and flexible even after five hours in the field? Or one that gets hard and leathery quickly and must be heated up to be eaten later? Does the grain swell sufficiently when cooked so that fewer ears are needed to feed the family?. . . Is it the kind that can be ground to a fine enough consistency for use in the preparation of the special chocolate drink?

—from *Cognitive Studies of Southern Mesoamerica*
* *Middle or Central America*

Buying Groceries

On the first day of our most recent trip to Guatemala City, we visited friends who live in a lower-income zone of the city. Next to their home was a little store with shelves on the back wall behind a wooden counter. The shopkeeper handed us two tiny tins of sardines while we picked out further purchases from the miniature boxes and cans of food. No economy sizes here, I thought, and suggested that we stop at a modern supermarket across town to finish our shopping.

As the man made change from three plastic dishes on a rickety table, a young woman dressed in a *huipil* and wraparound *corte** slipped up to the counter. I noticed her staring at our small mound of groceries and at the amount of money being returned to us. She placed a coin on the counter and mumbled a few words to the man. We picked up our groceries as the shopkeeper wrapped the woman's order in a piece of brown paper. She followed us out of the store, carrying one frankfurter.

—Guatemala City, July 1989   * See glossary

Tortilla Soup

12 tortillas
3 chile peppers
2 large onions, peeled
10 ripe cooking tomatoes

1 garlic clove
grated cheese (parmesan)
mint leaves
salt

Cut tortillas in thin strips and fry in oil. Separately, prepare tomato sauce: place whole tomatoes, 1 onion, 1 garlic clove, and chiles in a small amount of water. Boil till tomatoes are bursting and the onion, garlic, and chiles are tender. Blend well and pass through strainer. Cut the other onion in slices and sauté in a small amount of butter or margerine. When onion is golden, add tomato sauce; sauté a couple of minutes, and add the tortilla strips. Add salt to taste, and the mint leaves, chopped or whole as desired. Simmer briefly to thicken the sauce. To serve, sprinkle with cheese.

Chilaquila

8 tortillas
4 oz. cheese (cheddar or jack)
2 eggs
1 T. flour
salt to taste

Place cheese inside tortillas; fold in half. Beat egg whites until stiff, add egg yolks, flour, salt. Dip tortillas in egg mixture and fry in salad oil.

Toasted Tortillas with Hot Sauce

6 tomatoes
2 onions, peeled
1 chili pepper (or tabasco sauce)
salt

shortening or oil
grated cheese
parsley, chopped
tortillas

Cook tomatoes, onions, and chili pepper until soft. Mash or grind. Add salt to taste. Fry tortillas in deep oil until browned. To serve, cover tortillas with sauce and garnish with grated cheese and chopped parsley.

—Kitchen Fiesta

LOVE OF CHILDREN

Like the Dew

The laughter of children is like water
that falls slowly
upon the flowers.

The laughter of children
is like the warbling
of the *jilguero**
in the morning.

It is like the warmth
of the early sun
that kisses the fields
very softly.
> —Marilena López
> from *Poemas Escogidos
> para Niños*

* A brown bird with a red spot
on its head and a white collar

A Mayan Woman's Prayer

One common thread in the tapestry of life for the average Indian woman is the death of a child either at birth or within the first year of life. Pain is the same in any language.

Little flower of my womb,
image of your father,
portrait of your mother,
Why are you going
so far away?
Why do you leave me
in loneliness?
Why does your heart
no longer beat?
Did I not give you life
at the cost of my own
pain and suffering?
I nursed you at my breast,
I gave you food.
I protected you from birth.
Where is your sainted soul?
Why have you gone from me?
My heart is parting in two,
my heart grows weak,
my heart is prostrate and heavy
because of your death.
Your leaving is destroying me,
my little child, my little bird.
Where are you?
Little flower of my womb,
my heart is lonely
and calls for your
companionship.

—Daniel Jensen, M.M.
from *Revista Maryknoll*, November 1989[2]

HUMOR BORN OUT OF SUFFERING

Voting Irregularity:

Weeks before elections, a joke cropped up in Guatemala City: A little girl was crying, and her aunt asked her why. "Because Daddy didn't come to see me," she replied.

"But he died two years ago."

"Yes," the little girl said, "but they told me he voted yesterday."

—from *Guatemala: Eternal Spring, Eternal Tyranny*

From Bad to Worse:

After an outburst of violence, people have been heard to say, "Guatemala is now Guatepeor."

A Common Greeting:

"You're still alive?"

CAUSE FOR SORROW, CAUSE FOR HOPE

In an honest presidential ballot in 1985, Christian Democrat Vinicio Cerezo was elected. Although he enjoyed widespread popular support at the outset of his term, Cerezo has not tried to go beyond the limits set on his power by the military. The government under his leadership has not only refused to investigate past human rights abuses, it has failed to prevent new ones. Guatemala has a military government with a civilian face.[3]

Random Opinions (July 1989)

QUESTION: *What do you think about the present political situation in Guatemala?*

A baker from Italy, living in Guatemala for thirty-two years: The government is corrupt and there is political intrigue, just as in many other countries. Guatemalan government officials receive money from the United States and Europe that should be used to help the poor, but it just goes to make a few people rich and more powerful.

A twenty-year-old worker in the fish market: People don't have respect for our president (Cerezo). They say he's never in his office, and already he's settling his family in Washington before he goes out of office in the coming election. And the poor still suffer injustice.

A priest from the United States, in Guatemala for twenty-five years: I'm far from optimistic.

A fifty-year-old day laborer: If you are talking about our president, he is not sincere. He says one thing to the people and then does just the opposite. He's just filling his own pockets.

Young woman, missionary, in Guatemala for eight years: There's so much instability in all of Central America. We just take it one day at a time.

A middle-aged taxi driver: The economic situation is bad because the politicians favor the rich. Last night the president ordered the military to crack down on the teachers who are striking. Over a hundred teachers were beaten, arrested, and now are in jail or in the hospital. The politicians gave themselves a big raise, but the teachers are not supposed to ask for a small increase.

Young security guard at a hotel: Difficult, very difficult.

Young taxi driver: No matter how good this president, the military still is in control, so he can do nothing.

Well-to-do businessman: We are much better off now with a more democratic government. Everyone is allowed to express any opinion. Just look at the teacher and student demonstrations today. Of course, the government can't afford to raise the teachers' salaries because then they would have to raise the government workers' pay. We can't do that. Guatemala is a poor country.

Evangelical pastor: This president has done much more than people give him credit for, like paving streets, electrification of rural areas, and telephones. He has kept inflation down. These teachers on strike don't know how good they have it under this administration. Such disturbances can be the excuse the military will have to take over again.

Older U.S. citizen, married to a Guatemalan: According to my wife and her relatives, no one likes this president. I think the next president will be from the military.

A young man, director of a primary school: Things have stabilized somewhat. We have more tourism now, but it will take at least thirty years to establish a democratic government.

Teacher/student demonstration, Guatemala City, July 1989. Photo: M. Caldwell.

El Campesino Sigue Sembrando

Letra y Musica: Alvin Schutmaat, San Jose, C.R., 1983

The Farmer Keeps Sowing

Chorus:
(Estribillo): The seed falls. The seed will fall.
The seed keeps falling.
The Good News falls on good soil,
and the farmer keeps on sowing.

1: The Good News falls on the ground.
It falls among stones.
It falls among thorns.
But it also falls on good soil.

2: The good earth will produce fruit.
The time will come for the harvest.
The good earth will yield its harvest.
The day of justice will come soon.

3: The good earth, the good earth,
Is the earth of the laborer.
The good earth belongs to the people.
It is God's earth.

4: The people are earth, the earth is people.
From earth God makes the people.
They come from earth, to earth they return.
God breathed life into earth.

5: When the seed falls in good earth,
Then the world begins to change.
In earth thirsting for love and justice,
the farmer will keep sowing.

—Alvin Schutmaat,* Costa Rica, 1983

* Alvin Schutmaat, a Presbyterian missionary, assisted Latin American churches
to create hymns and songs with music indigenous to their cultures. He and
his wife, Pauline, served several years as consultants in music and the arts
to Central American churches. Used by permission of Pauline Schutmaat.

71

COMMON THREADS WITH CENTRAL AMERICA
To Oscar Romero

The ceiba tree and the quetzal are found not only in Guatemala, but in several tropical regions of Central America. Common to each country is the cry for freedom, the call for justice, the quest for a decent life for all, and a hope that cannot be extinguished.

Oscar Romero, the martyred archbishop of San Salvador, has become a symbol of hope for all those who suffer in Latin America. He was a pastorally minded prelate who grew in awareness of the suffering and poverty of his people and finally realized that he had to speak out against the civil war that was costing so many innocent lives. He rejected the charge that he was meddling in politics, declaring that he was "preaching the gospel as it should be preached for our people in this conflict-ridden reality." For such outspokenness, he was branded a Communist and assassinated while celebrating Mass.[4]

O towering, flowering ceiba tree,
roots sunk in earth,
soul bound for sky,
You vibrated with the spirit-wind
and we listened for your song.
But your resounding music
annoyed the forest keepers.
When springtime came,
they cut you down.
You crashed to the earth
and the power of your fall
Reverberated
Till a thousand thousand growing things
smaller than you,
but green—
so green—
began to tremble too.
Day on day their music swells
and fills the silent places.

The grim woodsmen stare.

All their axes multiplied
cannot still your song.

—Theodora Doleski, from *Revista Maryknoll*, March 1989[5]

A GUATEMALAN POSTSCRIPT

In spite of persecution, suffering, and often attempted annihilation during the last five hundred years, the Amerindians of Guatemala have survived, have maintained their cultural identity, and have remained the majority of the population. They have done more than survive: they have shown an ability and potential to recover what originally belonged to them.

The Indians' closeness to God's creation, their knowledge of God through nature, their strong community oriented culture, their commitment to each other, and their undefeated dignity are some of the evidences of hope and a brighter future.

The restoration of God's image among the poor and the needy is a difficult mission. More than human intervention is needed, however, if that restoration is to become a reality. God's love and faithfulness, expressed through God's people, are a source of encouragement and empowerment for the poor and the oppressed. This is a primary resource, one that many fighters for social change do not possess.

As God's people respond in obedience to the call to serve the needy and the suffering, they find endless opportunities to contribute to the expansion of the kingdom of God. The efforts of all people, Christian and non-Christian, are needed in this struggle for justice.

Jesus Christ and his liberating gospel are the best hope for my people.

—Alfonso Ayala, Jr.*

*Alfonso Ayala, Jr., is a medical doctor from Guatemala working in Belize. He is the son of Alfonso and Lucy Ayala, whose interview is on page 56.

Organizations Working to Help Guatemala

In the United States:

Central American Peace Institute
c/o Church of the Saviour
2025 Massachusetts Ave., NW
Washington, DC 20036

The Guatemalan Health Rights Support Project
1747 Connecticut Ave., NW
Washington, DC 20009
(202) 332-7678

Network in Solidarity with the
People of Guatemala (NISCUA)
1314 14th St., NW
Washington, DC 20005

Pueblo to People 1989
Field Guide to Citizen Diplomacy
1616 Montrose #3500
Houston, TX 77006

PEACE for Guatemala
P.O. Box 41740
Philadelphia, PA 19101-9706

Women for Guatemala
P.O. Box 53421
Washington, DC 20009

In Canada:

American Latina al Dia CFRO Radio (CFRO-FM)
337 Carroll St.
Vancouver, BC V6B 2J4

Amnesty International
Canadian Section, English Speaking
130 Slater St., Suite 800
Ottawa, Ontario KlP 6E2

Central America Information Group
81 Prince St.
Charlottetown, PEI C1A 4R3

Inter-Church Committee on Human
Rights in Latin America (ICCHRLA)
40 St. Clair Ave. East, #201
Toronto, Ontario M4T 1M9

Social Justice Center
2338 St. Antoine St. West
Montreal, Quebec H3J 1A8

Latin America Working Group
Box 2207, Station P
Toronto, Ontario M5S 2T2

Toronto Guatemala Solidarity Committee
Box 421, Station F
Toronto, Ontario M4Y 2L8

Glossary

alcalde (ahl-CAHL-day): mayor
altiplano (ahl-tee-PLAH-no): mountain plateau
caballerías (cah-bah-yeh-REE-ahs): agrarian measure of 96 acres
campesinos (cahm-pay-SEE-nos): farmers
Chiapas (Chee-AH-pahs): state in southern Mexico
corte (COR-tay): material used for wrap-around skirt
fincas (FEEN-cahs): farms
fucsia (FOO-see-ah): the color fuchsia
Huehuetenango (way-way-tay-NAHN-go): city in Guatemala near border of Mexico
huipiles (we-PEEL-ace): hand-woven blouses
ladinos (lah-DEE-nos): westernized, Spanish-speaking Indians
la migra (lah ME-grah): the immigration officials
Montt (Moant): General Efrain Rios Montt, an evangelical Protestant, became president through a coup in 1982 and ruled for eighteen of the bloodiest months in modern Guatemalan history.
niños (NEEN-yose): children

Recommended Resources

Books

Americas Watch. "Guatemala: A Nation of Political Prisoners." New York: Americas Watch Report, 1984.

Anderson, Marilyn. *Granddaughters of Corn.* Willamantic, Connecticut: Curbstone Press, 1988.

Carmack, Robert M., ed. *Harvest of Violence: The Maya Indians and the Guatemalan Crisis.* Norman, Oklahoma: University of Oklahoma Press, 1988.

Handy, Jim. *Gift of the Devil: A History of Guatemala.* Boston: South End Press, 1984.

Kinzer, Stephen and Stephen Schlesinger. *Bitter Fruit: The Untold Story of the American Coup in Guatemala.* Garden City, New York: Anchor Books, 1983.

Montejo, Victor. *Testimony: Death of a Guatemalan Village.* Willamantic: Connecticut: Curbstone, Press, 1987.

Nouwen, Henri J.M. *Love in a Fearful Land: A Guatemalan Story.* Notre Dame, Indiana: Ave Maria Press, 1985.

Painter, James. *Guatemala: False Hope, False Freedom.* London: Latin American Bureau, 1987.

Perera, Victor. *Rites: A Guatemalan Boyhood.* New York: Harcourt Brace Jovanovich, 1986.

See also items starred * in the Index to Sources.

Photographs

Granddaughters of Corn. See Books list above. Photos by Marilyn Anderson.

Guatemala: Eternal Spring, Eternal Tyranny. See Index to Sources. Almost 100 striking color photographs accompany the text, both by Jean-Marie Simon.

"Sight Unseen: Photographs of Guatemala'"'is an exhibit of 35 black and white photographs by three professional photographers who document the people, pain and politics of Guatemala: Derrill Bazzy and Pat Goodvis (some of their photographs are reproduced in this scrapbook) and Jerry Berndt. The exhibit is mounted and captioned, and may be rented for up to three weeks. (A 70-photo exhibit by 5 photographers is also available.) Send inquiries to Oxfam America Photo Exhibit, 115 Broadway, Boston, MA 02116 (telephone: 617-482-1211).

AYUDA publishers calendars with stunning black and white photos. The Guatemala 1989 calendar focuses on refugees and the 1990 calendar on "women of courage." Calendars list important Central American dates and also explain the Mayan calendar. Funds from calendar support organizations of refugees, women, etc. Calendars available through AYUDA, P.O. Box 1752, Boston, MA 02105. 1-4 copies, $8 each; 5-24 copies, $6.50 each; includes shipping.

Illustrations

Page iv. Guatemalan woman and child. Photo by Pat Goodvis.

Page 7. Under a ceiba tree. Photo by Maurice Caldwell.

Pages 11-12. Guatemalan textile depicting marimba players. Photo by George Abiad.

Page 17. Quetzal, drawing by a Guatemalan in exile. Illustration from *Threatened with Resurrection*, by Julia Esquivel. Elgin, Ill.: The Brethren Press, 1982. Used by permission of Brethren Press.

Page 20. Central American volcano. United Nations photo 85875.

Page 32. Gloria Ortiz for "Call This Witness 'Sanctuary,'" *New Conversations* (Vol. 9, No. 2, Summer 1986), the United Church Board For Homeland Ministries.

Page 34. Worshippers in Chichicastenango burn incense in a religious ritual on the steps of Santo Tomas church. United Nations photo 131,962/Jerry Frank.

Page 38. Replicas of costumed dancers, at the National Museum in Guatemala City. Photo by Maurice Caldwell.

Page 43. Church in San Mateo. United Nations photo 152,289/Antoinette Jongen.

Page 49. Detail of photo by Derill Bazzy

Page 53. UN/UNDP photo 155664/C. Blomqvist

Page 54. Photo of Lucy Ayala by Maurice Caldwell.

Page 56. Concepción Ramírez. Painting by Rebeca Calderón.

Page 57. The likeness of Concepción Ramírez on a twenty-five-cent coin. Photo by George Abiad.

Page 63. In Santiago Atitlán, a woman begins the weaving process by making thread. Photo by Derrill Bazzy, 1985.

Page 65. Making tortillas from corn dough. Photo by Maurice Caldwell.

Page 66. Children in San Mateo. United Nations photo 152,280/Antoinette Jongen.

Page 69. Teacher/student demonstration. Photo by Maurice Caldwell.

Page 73. "Fortunate are those who have the spirit of the poor, for theirs is the kingdom of Heaven," from a series illustrating the Beatitudes, by Maximino Cerezo Barredo. Used by permission of Claretian Publications, Quezon City, P.I.

Index to Sources

Friendship Press is grateful to the following publishers, authors and photographers for permission to reprint selections, which are listed as titled in this book.
*Recommended Reading

Books

Cognitive Studies of Southern Mesoamerica, Publication 3, by Helen Neuenswander and Dean E. Arnold. Guatemala City: Summer Institute of Linguistics, 1977. From pages 10-14, 96-98, 99-100. Reprinted with permission of author and publisher.

"Prayers Before the Dance," page 38.
"Corn, the Essence of Life," page 64.

Footloose Scientist in Maya America, by Mary Corde Lorang. New York: Curtis Brown Ltd./Scribner & Sons, 1966. From pages 105, 108. Reprinted by permission of Curtis Brown, Ltd. Copyright 1966 by Maryknoll Sisters of St. Dominic, Inc.

"Want to Buy a Machete?" page 49.

Four Keys to Guatemala, by Vera Kelsey and Lilly de Jongh Osborne. New York: Funk & Wagnalls, Reader's Digest Press, 1961. From pages 31, 32, 35, 47, 58, 59, 78. Copyright 1961 by Vera Kelsey. Reprinted by permission of Harper & Row, Publishers, Inc.

"Some Indian Beliefs and Practices," page 39.
"The Black Christ of Esquipulas," page 39.
"Buying Land We Already Own," page 48.
"Textiles and Prayer," page 61.

Guatemala: Eternal Spring, Eternal Tyranny, by Jean-Marie Simon. New York: Norton, 1987. Quotations used by permission of W.W. Norton and Co., Inc. Copyright © 1987 by Jean-Marie Simon.

Quote from Archbishop Penados, page 25.
Quote under heading "An Army Informant," page 28.
"Who in Your Family Has 'Disappeared'?" page 30.
"The Land Is So Good," page 37.
"Christians or Communists?" page 41.
"Catholics or Protestants?" page 42.
"Voting Irregularity," page 68.

Amnesty International, "Guatemala: Human Rights Violations Reported Under the Administration of President Vinicio Cerezo Arévalo (January 1986—Present)," April 1987 report. Used by permission of A.I. Quote under "Speaking Out," page 29.

I, Rigoberta Menchu, by Rigoberta Menchú, edited by Elisabeth Burgos-Debray. New York: Verso, The Alpine Press, 1984. From pages 1, 8, 15, 116, 172, 178, 179, 246, 247, 132-135, 80. Reprinted by permission of the publisher.

"Always Our Home," quote from *Popul Vuh*, page 11.
"The Birth of a Child," page 18.
"The Root of Our Problem," page 28
"False Accusation, Torture, Death," page 28.
"Religion and Culture," page 41.
"Faith and Poverty," page 43.
"Statement of Beliefs," page 44.
"Textiles and the Person," page 61.

Kitchen Fiesta, a cookbook compiled by the Women's Auxiliary of The Union Church of Guatemala, 1981. By permission of the Auxiliary.

Recipes for Tortilla Soup, Toasted Tortillas, and Chilaquila, page 65.

Poemas Escogidos, para Niños, edited by Francisco Morales Santos. Guatemala City: Editorial Piedra Santa, 1987. From pages 50, 88, 89, 113,115, 117, 179. Reprinted by permission of the publisher. Translations here by Dondeena Caldwell.

"La Ceiba de Mi Pueblo," page 7.

"Monja Blanca," pages 8, 9.

"La Ceiba," pages 8, 9.

"A Guatemala," page 10.

"15 de Septiembre," page 12.

"El Quetzal," page 17.

"Razones del Maíz," pages 18,19.

"Like the Dew," page 66.

Ritual Rhetoric from Cotzal, compiled by Paul G. Townsend. Guatemala City: Instituto Linguistico de Verano, 1980. From pages v., 17-18. Reprinted by permission of the publisher.

"Broken Bone Healing Ritual Prayer," page 40.

*Threatened with Resurrection, by Julia Esquivel. Elgin, IL: The Brethren Press, 1982. Pages 45-49, 106-109. Reprinted by permission of the publisher.

"The Wounded Quetzal," pages 26, 27.

"Indian Tapestry," pages 62, 63.

*Unexpected News: Reading the Bible Through Third World Eyes, by Robert McAfee Brown. Philadelphia: Westminster Press, 1984. From pages 152-153. Copyright © 1984 by Robert McAfee Brown. Used by permission of Westminster/John Knox Press.

"Base Community," page 44.

The View from the Top of the Temple, by Kenneth Pearce. Albuquerque: University of New Mexico Press, 1984. From pages 71, 270. Used by permission of the publisher.

"God of Thunder and Lightening," page 20.

"The Huipil," page 58.

*The Wounded Quetzal: Women and Weaving in Guatemala, edited by Gayle Boss and Cherly Hellner. Potter's House Press, P.O. Box 21039, Washington, DC 20009, 1987. From Vol 2, No. 1. The following excerpts are reprinted by permission of the publisher; © 1987 by Potter's House Press.

"Lament," quoted from *Annals of the Cakchiquel,* page 28.

Quote from Lily de Jongh Osborne in introduction to Chapter 5, page 45.

Quote from *Popul Vuh,* page 58.

Words of a Mayan weaver in "Textiles and the Military," page 61.

Magazines: See Footnotes for complete references.

Christianity and Crisis, 537 West 121st St., New York, NY 10027. Copyright July 10, 1989.

"Catholics and Protestants Working Together," page 42

Maryknoll and *Revista Maryknoll,* Maryknoll, NY 10545.

"Our Father for Today," page 36.

"A Mayan Woman's Prayer," page 67.

The Other Side, 300 W. Apsley St., Philadelphia, PA 19144. $21.75 per year. Copyright March 1985, November 1987.

Adaptation in introduction to Chapter Three, pages 21, 22.

"Sanctuary," page 32.

"Me Llamo Mateo: A Peasant's Lament," pages 52, 53.

Sojourners, Box 29272, Washington, DC 20017.

"Refugees/Chiapas," page 31.

Poems and Photographs: For complete references, see Footnotes and Illustrations

Theodora Doleski for "To Oscar Romero," © 1989 by Theodora Doleski Petosa, page 72.

Cheryl Kolander for "This I Ask Ye," pages 23, 25.

Pat Goodvis for photographs on pages iv, 24, 59.

Derrill Bazzy for photographs on pages 4, 14, 46, 49, 63.

Footnotes

One: The Sacred Land of the Mayas

1. Anne LaBastille Bowers, "The Quetzal," *National Geographic*, Vol. 135, No. 1 (Jan. 1969), p. 141.
2. Vera Kelsey and Lilly de Jongh Osborne, *Four Keys to Guatemala* (New York: Funk & Wagnalls, Reader's Digest Books, 1961), p. 111.
3. Kelsey and Osborne, *Four Keys*, p. 5.
4. Kelsey and Osborne, *Four Keys*, p. 22
5. Kenneth Pearce, *The View from the Top of the Temple* (Albuquerque: Univ. of New Mexico Press, 1984), p. 194.
6. David C. Whitney Associates, Inc., *1980 Almanac and Yearbook* (Pleasantville, Reader's Digest Ass'n., 1980), p. 562.
7. Pearce, *The View*, p. 195.
8. Kelsey and Osborne, *Four Keys*, p. 116.

Two: From Corn Paste to Kings

1. Vera Kelsey and Lilly de Jongh Osborne, *Four Keys to Guatemala* (New York: Funk & Wagnalls, Reader's Digest Books, 1961), p. 100.
2. Kelsey and Osborne, *Four Keys*, pp. 5-6.
3. Kenneth Pearce, *The View from the Top of the Temple* (Albuquerque; Univ. of New Mexico Press, 1984), p. 201.
4. Herbert Wendt, *The Red, White, and Black Continent* (New York: Doubleday, 1966), p. 108. Translation copyright © by Doubleday, a division of Bantam Doubleday Dell Publishing Group Inc. Reprinted by permission of the publisher.
5. Gayle Boss and Cheryl Hellner, eds., *The Wounded Quetzal: Women and Weaving in Guatemala*, Vol. 2, No. 1, (Washington, DC: Potter's House Press, 1987), p. 2.
6. Helda Cole Espey with Les Creamer, Jr., *Another World: Central America* (New York: Viking, 1970), p. 135.
7. *Popul Vuh* passage translated from Gerardo Gordillo Barrios, *Guatemala Historia Gráfica* (Guatemala: Editorial Piedra Santa, 1982), pp. 92-92.
8. Wilbur E. Garrett, "La Ruta Maya," *National Geographic*, Vol. 176, No. 4 (Oct. 1989), p. 440.

Three: If Quetzals Could Cry

1. Daniel Spencer, "The Army Remains: A Short History of Guatemala," in *The Other Side* (Nov. 1987), p. 21.

2. Jane P. Keegan, RDC, *Third World Peoples: Focus on Central America* curriculum (Maryknoll, NY: Maryknoll Fathers and Brothers, 1987), pp. 42, 44.
3. Gayle Boss and Cheryl Hellner, eds. *The Wounded Quetzal*, Vol 2, No. 1, (Washington, DC: Potter's House Press, 1987), p. 19.
4. Richard Fagen, *Forging Peace: The Challenge of Central America* (London & New York: Basil Blackwell, 1987), p. 94.
5. Fagen, *Forging Peace*, p. 95.
6. "This I Ask Ye" is reprinted with the kind permission of the author. The poem first appeared in *Interweavings* magazine in 1981.
7. Stacie Smith Rowe, "Refugees/ Chiapas" in *Sojourners* (Dec, 1984).
8. Michael McConnell, "Sanctuary: No Stopping Now," in *The Other Side* (Mar. 1985), p. 33.

Four: From Gods to God
1. Kenneth Pearce, *The View from the Top of the Temple* (Albuquerque: Univ. of New Mexico Press, 1984), p. 71.
2. Vera Kelsey and Lilly de Jongh Osborne, *Four Keys to Guatemala* (New York: Funk & Wagnalls, Reader's Digest Books, 1961), p. 223.
3. Pearce, *The View*, p. 211.
4. Kelsey and Osborne, *Four Keys*, p. 20.
5. Hartley Burr Alexander, *The Mythology of All Races; Vol. XI, Latin America* (Totowa, NJ: Cooper Square Publishers, 1964), pp. 142-3.
6. Richard F. Nyrop, *Guatemala: A Country Study* (Washington, DC: American University, May 1983), p. 68.
7. Nyrop, *Guatemala*, p. 72.
8. Guatemala News and Information Bureau, "The Rise of the Religious Right in Central America," in *Report on Gautemala*, Vol. 8, Issue 5 (Nov.-Dec. 1985), pp. 7, 12.
9. Richard Fagen, *Forging Peace: The Challenge of Central America* (London & New York: Basil Blackwell, 1987), p. 91.
10. Nyrop, *Guatemala*, p. 75.
11. Rosemary Radford Ruether, "Ecumenism in Central America," in *Christianity and Crisis* (July 10, 1989), p. 212.
12. Robert McAfee Brown, *Theology in a New Key* (Philadelphia: Westminster, 1978), p. 172.
13. "Our Father for Today" from *Maryknoll,*, Vol. 83, No. 5 (May 1989), pp. 60-62.
14. Ruether, "Ecumenism In Central America," p. 209.

Five: A Living Tapestry
1. Gayle Boss and Cheryl Hellner, eds. *The Wounded Quetzal*, Vol 2, No. 1 (Washington, DC: Potter's House Press, 1987), p. 8.
2. Vera Kelsey and Lilly de Jongh Osborne, *Four Keys to Guatemala* (New York: Funk & Wagnalls, Reader's Digest Books, 1961), p. 84.
3. Jane P. Keegan, RDC, *Third World People: Focus on Central America* curriculum (Maryknoll, NY: Maryknoll Fathers and Brothers, 1987), p. 42.
4. Daniel Spencer, "Me Llamo Mateo: A Peasant's Lament," *The Other Side* (Nov. 1987), p. 17.

Six: Threads of the Tapestry
1. Vera Kelsey and Lilly de Jongh Osborne, *Four Keys to Guatemala* (New York: Funk & Wagnalls, Reader's Digest Books, 1961), p. 80.
2. Daniel Jensen, M.M., "A Mayan Woman's Prayer," in *Revista Maryknoll*, Sociedad Católica de América para Misiones Extranjeras, Inc., Vol 8, No. 11 (Nov. 1989), pp. 26-27.
3. Richard Fagen, *Forging Peace: The Challenge of Central America* (London & New York: Basil Blackwell, 1987), pp. 88, 93.
4. Ronald Saucci, M.M., in *Maryknoll* magazine, Vol 83, No. 9 (Sept. 1989), p. 44.
5. Theodora Doleski, "To Oscar Romero," *Revista Maryknoll*, Vol. 10, No. 3 (Mar. 1989), p. 71.

A KISS FOR LITTLE BEAR

An I CAN READ Book®

by ELSE HOLMELUND MINARIK

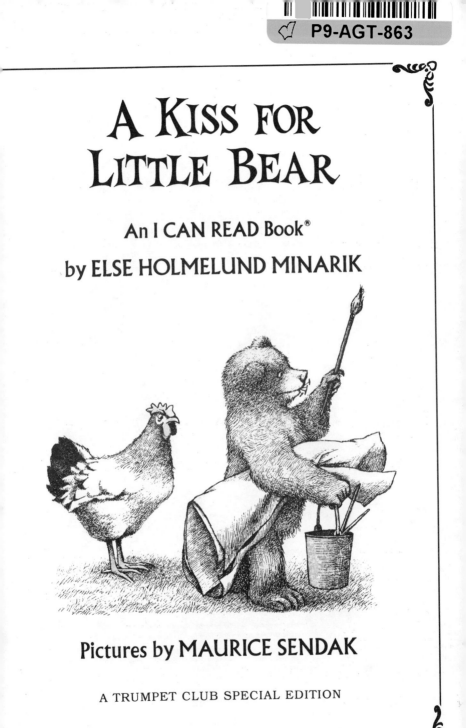

Pictures by MAURICE SENDAK

A TRUMPET CLUB SPECIAL EDITION

Published by The Trumpet Club
666 Fifth Avenue New York, New York 10103

Text copyright © 1968 by Else Holmelund Minarik
Illustrations copyright © 1968 by Maurice Sendak

The trademark Dell® is registered in the U.S. Patent and Trademark Office.
ISBN: 0-440-84097-X

Reprinted by arrangement with Harper & Row, Publishers, Inc.
Printed in the United States of America   October 1989

10 9 8 7 6 5 4 3 2 1 UPC

A KISS FOR LITTLE BEAR

"This picture makes me happy,"

said Little Bear.

"Hello, Hen.

This picture is for Grandmother.

Will you take it to her, Hen?"

"Yes, I will," said Hen.

Grandmother was happy.

"This kiss is for Little Bear," she said.

"Will you take it to him, Hen?"

"I will be glad to," said Hen.

Then Hen saw some friends.

She stopped to chat.

"Hello, Frog.

I have a kiss for Little Bear.

It is from his grandmother.

Will you take it to him, Frog?"

"OK," said Frog.

But Frog saw a pond.

He stopped to swim.

"Hi, Cat.

I have a kiss for Little Bear.

It is from his grandmother.

Take it to him, will you?

Cat—hi!

Here I am, in the pond.

Come and get the kiss."

"Oogh!" said Cat.

But he came and got the kiss.

Cat saw a nice spot to sleep.

"Little Skunk,

I have a kiss for Little Bear.

It is from his grandmother.

Take it to him like a good little skunk."

Little Skunk was glad to do that.

But then he saw another little skunk.

She was very pretty.

He gave the kiss to her.

And she gave it back.

And he gave it back.

And then Hen came along.

"Too much kissing," she said.

"But this is Little Bear's kiss,

from his grandmother,"

said Little Skunk.

"Indeed!" said Hen.

"Who has it now?"

Little Skunk had it.

Hen got it back.

She ran to Little Bear,

and she gave him the kiss.

"It is from your grandmother,"

she said.

"It is for the picture you sent her."

"Take one back to her,"

said Little Bear.

"No," said Hen.

"It gets all mixed up!"

The skunks decided to get married.

They had a lovely wedding.

Everyone came.

And Little Bear was best man.